No. 9

MARKETING BELOW-THE-LINE

Studies in Management

MARKETING
BELOW-THE-LINE

MARTIN CHRISTOPHER
in association with
Donald Cowell
Michael Morris
Gordon Wills

Foreword by Professor Gordon Wills

London
GEORGE ALLEN & UNWIN LTD
RUSKIN HOUSE   MUSEUM STREET

16742

First published in 1972

© George Allen & Unwin Ltd 1972

ISBN 0 04 658073 5

Printed in Great Britain by
Alden & Mowbray Ltd
at the Alden Press, Oxford

Before, behind, between, above, below

John Donne, 1593

CONTENTS

THE BRADFORD/HORNIBLOW, COX-FREEMAN STUDY

In October 1968 work started within the Marketing Communications Research Unit at the University of Bradford Management Centre on a research programme into the phenomenon
of below-the-line promotion in the United Kingdom. This study,
the most thorough and extensive undertaken in the area, was
originated by Horniblow, Cox-Freeman, a leading British
advertising agency (now a part of Benton & Bowles Ltd which
is itself a subsidiary of the international advertising agency,
Benton & Bowles Inc.). Specifically the aims of the study were:

To conduct a two, to two and a half-year investigation of
below-the-line promotion, in order to chart what has taken
place and to develop its rationale as a basis for effective
current and future use.
The study starts from the premise that below-the-line
promotional activity in Britain has passed through the introductory stage of its development cycle. What exactly has
happened during this phase is imprecisely understood. This
undermines the efforts of advertising/promotional agencies
and marketing management to deploy below-the-line promotion both now and in the future.

In July 1969 the preliminary desk-research investigation into
the state of knowledge of below-the-line promotion was
published.[1] As a result of that survey, it was possible to define
more clearly the areas where knowledge was thin and further
research needed. It was decided that the next stage of the
research programme should be three-pronged: first, to determine consumers' attitudes towards below-the-line generally,
and their preferences amongst the various types of promotion

[1] *An Investigation into the Below-the-line promotion Industry in the U.K.* (Management
Centre, Bradford, 1969).

available; secondly, to investigate the opinions of retailers on the effectiveness of these various promotions in moving goods off the shelf; and finally to conduct a number of in-depth studies of manufacturers who had experience below-the-line.

This book represents the culmination of these efforts and, in addition to reporting the findings of the survey carried out by Unit Market Search Ltd, it draws together the related, albeit sparse, literature on the subject. More than this, however, *Marketing Below-the-Line* examines the role of below-the-line promotion in the total company and marketing environment and suggests possible improvements over present practice.

Marketing Below-the-Line is the first of a number of projected reports describing the research findings of the University of Bradford Management Centre's Marketing Communications Research Unit. This Unit, supported by eighteen major U.K. and international companies, is currently concerned with research into methods of evaluating the effectiveness of advertising. This further programme of work has been made possible by the efforts of Bradford's Visiting Professor of Marketing, Harry Henry. A central theme of the work of this Unit is its emphasis on the need to take a 'total' view of corporate communications—a point of view echoed strongly in this book.

The initiative for the study described in this book lay with one advertising agency, Horniblow, Cox-Freeman who recognized the possibly dramatic impact on traditional agency business of the growth in below-the-line. The particular pattern of Agency/Business School co-operation that followed has formed a model for the further profitable fusion of theory and practice in other areas. It is possible in areas such as these to achieve a desirable synergy between the agency's need to know something of the underlying processes in a marketing phenomenon and the Business School's continuing need for contact with operational situations.

GORDON WILLS
Professor of Marketing Studies
University of Bradford Management Centre

In preparing this book, I have relied heavily on the contributions of my associates, Don Cowell, Michael Morris, and Gordon Wills. Their ideas and active help have been a great stimulus to the thoughts embodied in these chapters.

Particular debt is owed to Horniblow, Cox-Freeman Ltd, now a part of Benton & Bowles, for setting up the study. I am also indebted to J. Walter Thompson Company Limited who, by allowing me the chance to work in the invigorating environment of 40 Berkeley Square in the summer of 1970, enabled the ground-work for this book to be laid.

M. G. C.

ACKNOWLEDGEMENTS

BELOW-THE-LINE PROMOTION AND THE ADVERTISING AGENCY

EVOLUTION in the marketing environment has made the advertising agency unique among marketing institutions. Financed not by the companies whose products it promotes but by the owners of the media it utilizes for this promotion, presenting a variety of services other than the traditional agency functions of creative formulation of advertisements and the buying of media space and time, the advertising agency occupies a precarious position between the manufacturers and the media.

The commission system that the majority of agencies rely on for their income means that their profitability is geared to the size of the manufacturers' appropriations. In thin times, when appropriations fall, the agency is hit hard, and in good times and in bad, the agency is expected to provide the advertiser with a whole host of specialist services for which an economic charge is rarely made. Thus the advertising agency tends to be squeezed from all directions, no matter what the economic climate may be.

More recently, a further source of profit erosion has appeared on the agencies' financial horizon. The growth of expenditure by manufacturers below rather than above-the-line has often meant that a diminishing slice of a not very fast-growing total appropriation has been available for expenditure on media advertising. This latter pressure on the agency has been interpreted by many agencies to be a threat to their existence, and a great number of such agencies have established subsidiary companies to deal exclusively with below-the-line promotion. Very few agencies have viewed the phenomenon as a challenge, and as an opportunity for a greater involvement in the advertiser's total communications activity.

It will be suggested later in this book that the future for the advertising agency lies in recognizing the true nature of its business and its relationship with clients—in other words, an acceptance of the concept of the agency as the creative catalyst in the client's total communications effort. Thus, the advertising agency under this paradigm is concerned not only with the skilful creation and placing of media advertising promoting a product or a company, but is concerned also with all the complementary promotional activity such as corporate design, merchandising, and below-the-line. Only in this way can a company and its products be given a contradiction-free 'personality' that is meaningful and relevant to its customers.

Needless to say, many advertising agencies would welcome this role but are thwarted to some extent by manufacturers who prefer to use separate agencies for what they perceive to be separate activities. Thus merchandising will often be contracted out to a specialist agency and below-the-line to another. There is nothing inherently wrong in this situation, but it is usually the case that there is no coherent and co-ordinated brief issue by the company which clearly states overall brand and company objectives. Quite clearly the responsibility for the adoption of a total approach to promotional planning lies with the manufacturer. There is a need for a detailed and integrated plan, in the form of promotional briefs, to emanate from the marketing department of the client company. Our researches for the preparation of this book have shown that this is rarely the case.

Reference was made earlier to the commission-basis of agency incomes. Traditionally, media owners have allowed a discount of 15 per cent to the agency on advertisements placed with them. No other fee is usually charged. Thus the advertising agency has only one major source of profit—the advertisements it places. The advertising profession has never been completely happy with this situation, but has argued that it is necessary in order that price-cutting does not become prevalent. The adherence to the principle has meant, however, that it is not possible within the conventional agency structure to handle anything other than media advertising. Integrated involvement in below-the-line by the agency would mean, to all intents and purposes, the abandonment of commissions in favour of a fee system.

In many cases, too, the internal organization of the advertising agency does not lend itself to an integrated approach to promotional planning. The organic growth and development of the agency has tended to be haphazard. A typical agency structure will have three distinct levels: primary, secondary, and tertiary (Figure 1).

This structure is not perfectly suited to an approach which essentially requires a definition of the brand's problems prepared jointly by client and agency, and a total multi-faceted approach to their solution. In a way, the recent trend towards the creation of breakaway 'boutique' agencies with a handful of personnel working as a team is more likely to provide a viable problem-solving framework. This movement is very much akin to the approach adopted by some of the more sophisticated marketing companies where their internal organization is structured along 'venture group' lines. Here a small group is responsible for the creation, development, testing and launching of a new product. They bring together a mixture of skills and cut across traditional functional lines to produce a highly involved and creative environment concerned with the problems of one brand. It should not be too difficult to translate this approach into the agency framework, the difference being that the 'venture group' would now be concerned with the total communications problem of the company for whom it is working.

Whatever the organizational solution, the need to break free from the present situation is apparent. Future changes in the marketing environment may be such that the traditional advertising agency may well be faced with the choice of adapting its role or losing it altogether.

THE NEED FOR RESEARCH BELOW-THE-LINE

In later chapters, frequent mention is made of the paucity of available research findings, qualitative and quantitative, relating to the whole field of below-the-line promotion. There cannot be many fields of management action today where decisions concerning the expenditure of massive sums of money are taken on the basis of so few hard research findings. Indeed, many companies appear to adopt a highly unsophisticated and

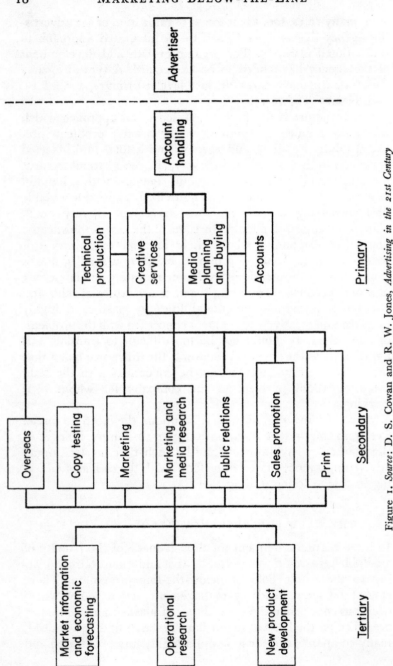

Figure 1. *Source:* D. S. Cowan and R. W. Jones, *Advertising in the 21st Century* (Hutchinson, London, 1968).

haphazard approach to the allocation of below-the-line expenditure.

To say that the form of promotion chosen should be salient to the needs of the product/market situation prevailing at the time may be a truism, but in fact there is little evidence of attempts being made to achieve such a salience. Yet the correct identification of this product/market situation can be crucial to the success of the promotion. The model (Figure 2) illustrates a possible, simplified approach to such an analysis.

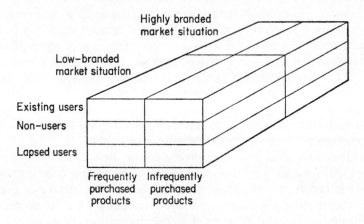

Figure 2

In this case, the product/market situation is examined at a given time in terms of just three dimensions. First, the nature of the consumers or the potential consumers, i.e. do they currently purchase the product; have they purchased the product in the past but not now; have they never purchased the product? Second, the nature of the purchase cycle: is the product frequently or infrequently purchased? Third, what is the nature of the market, i.e. is it a market typified by highly branded products or is branding less apparent? There could be other dimensions such as the purchase involving risk, economic or social, or a brand-loyalty dimension could be included, and so on.

In this example, there are obviously twelve possible product/ market situations, only a few of which will be the target for action. In addition to this, the company will presumably have adopted some global marketing strategy, for example, a policy of market penetration, i.e. selling more to its existing market, or a policy of market development, i.e. selling its existing product in new markets or new market segments. Thus, for each cell of our multi-dimensional matrix there could be alternative market ing and promotional strategies depending on the nature of the global strategy.

The importance of this approach should be clear. A different promotional strategy is called for if the company is attempting to increase penetration amongst existing users of a frequently purchased product in a highly branded market than if it was attempting to open up a new market amongst a segment of non-users of an infrequently purchased, low-branded product.

The formulation of such a promotional strategy and the determination of the most appropriate promotion for the situation is obviously a task calling for great creative skills. Unfortunately experience has shown that creativity in promotion tends to be the monopoly of media promotion.

Research can help the promoter by first identifying the product/market situation, and then by presenting cues for the formulation of an appropriate promotional strategy. For example, whilst it may not always be necessary for the promotion to make sense in terms of its relationship to the product, it must make sense in terms of the consumer's propensity to participate in that type of promotion. Research can often match the consumer to the promotion and thus enable a more rational approach to this aspect of below-the-line promotion to be adopted.

This then, is the background to *Marketing Below-the-Line*. The role of the traditional advertising agency *vis-à-vis* below-the-line must change if it is to take the fullest advantage of the potential offered by this promotional vehicle to the mutual benefit of the agency and the client. At the same time, there is a pressing need for a greater understanding of the dynamics of below-the-line promotion, an understanding which is most likely to come through rigorous research.

CHAPTER ONE

WHAT IS BELOW-THE-LINE?

THE 1960s witnessed a silent yet dramatic revolution, almost unheralded whilst in progress and only chronicled when it had passed its climax. This revolution was the growth of a form of promotional expenditure which came to be known as 'below-the-line'. It was below-the-line in the sense that it was not expenditure on promotion in the conventional and time-honoured form, i.e. advertising through the media of the press, cinema, television, and poster. It was, in fact, expenditure on sales promotions; promotions designed to have an impact, albeit short-term, on sales volume. These promotions typically have taken the form of offering either extra value for money in the form of money off, coupons, or free samples, or have attempted to generate excitement in the product through the vehicles of competitions, games, and give-aways.

There is nothing new about this form of promotion. It has been practised in one form or another since the late nineteenth century. What is new is the magnitude of activity in this area. Estimates (and they can only be estimates because of the problems of definition and measurement) of promotional expenditure below-the-line put a figure of between £350m. and £450m. spent annually in the years 1965–9, these figures including an estimate of the value of the goods offered in premium-type promotions. When this is compared with the figure of just under £500m. spent annually on media advertising, some measure of its relative importance may be gained.

A feature of even greater importance, at least to the traditional advertising agency, has been the fact that marketing appropriations have not grown as fast in recent years as the demands that have been made upon them. Thus the increase in the slice of cake going below-the-line has meant that the amount available for above-the-line has tended to shrink. Advertising agencies have found that they have had to run a lot harder in recent years to keep billings growing at a rate equivalent to the increase in costs. The late 1960s saw a large number of mergers and amalgamations between agencies as the competition increased. It is not an unreasonable assumption to suggest that part of this changed environment was due to the increase in below-the-line promotional activity during this period.

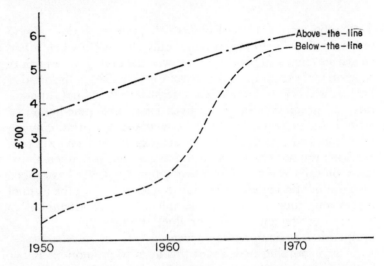

Figure 1.1. Composite estimates of relative promotional expenditures

Whilst definitions of the scope of below-the-line vary, for the purpose of consistency throughout this book the term 'below-the-line promotion' will be taken to mean 'all non-media promotion'. Included in this definition are trade schemes such as discounts, sales force incentives, and point-of-sale merchandising material. Any definition must necessarily be arbitrary to a point, and whilst this definition is adopted here, it may not be the best definition, organizationally speaking, for the individual company.

A useful distinction can be drawn between those promotions which are aimed at moving products from the marketing channel intermediary, for example, the retailer, to the consumer (called 'out-of-the-pipeline') and those concerned with

moving products from the manufacturer to the channel intermediary ('into-the-pipeline'). The typical manufacturer will
use both these approaches either broadscale across all his
brands and all selling outlets, or selectively, using his promotions on specific brands to solve specific marketing problems.

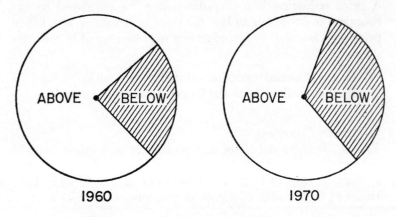

Figure 1.2. The promotional cake. How it was cut

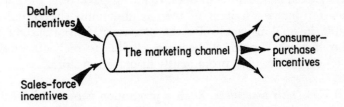

Figure 1.3. Selling into and out of the pipeline

Using this distinction between 'into' and 'out of the pipeline'
we may list the major forms of below-the-line promotion used
today.

SELLING OUT OF THE PIPELINE

1. *Free Samples*
With this type of promotion, the consumer receives a free
sample of the product either given away in store, or delivered

direct to households by agents. The consumer is not required to make payments of any sort, and is under no obligation to purchase the product on future occasions.

2. *Price Reductions*

A price reduction is a markdown in price employed to encourage the consumer to buy the same unit/volume at a lower price than normal. Price reductions may be offered to the consumer:

(i) By the manufacturer, i.e. printed on the pack.
(ii) By the retailer, i.e. in the form of store price cuts.

3. *Premium Promotions*

This is where an article of merchandise or any other thing of value is offered to the consumer as an inducement to purchase a product. It may be offered as a bonus or at a nominal charge. Included in this area of premium promotional activity are:

(i) *Free 'in/on/off-pack' offers*. With an 'in-pack' offer the manufacturer gives away an item such as a plastic toy, which is pre-packed inside the container. In an 'on-pack' offer the manufacturer bands an item of merchandise onto the container, while in an 'off-pack' offer the consumer, in purchasing the manufacturer's product, becomes eligible to pick up another item of merchandise prominently displayed in store.

(ii) *Personality promotions*. Such a promotion is one which offers cash or prizes either in-store or outside, for example, consumers are asked to produce packs of the manufacturer's product, and/ or quote a pre-promoted catch-phrase and/or use their skill and judgement to answer a question.

(iii) *Competitions*. Consumers are encouraged to use their skill and judgement in solving a promoted competition. As a condition of entry, participants may be required to send to the competition-promoters evidence of purchase of the product (for example, a container top) with their solution.

(iv) *Coupon offers*. The consumer is offered coupons, either distributed directly to households or on the product label, which enables her to obtain the manufacturer's product or another at a reduced price, or free.

(v) *Saving incentives.* These are incentives offered by the manufacturer or retailer to increase consumer purchases of their products. The two prime examples in the United Kingdom are trading stamps and cigarette gift coupons. When a sufficient number of stamps or coupons have been collected, they may be exchanged for cash or for gifts. These may be schemes run either by a single manufacturer (e.g. cigarette coupons), by a group of manufacturers offering compatible coupons or tokens on non-competing brands, or by stamp companies offering stamps usually in relation to the total value of purchases at a retail outlet.

(vi) *Self-liquidating offers.* Here merchandise is offered to consumers at less than retail price, but the margin to the manufacturer is such that he makes sufficient profit to cover all the costs of the promotion, i.e. the promotion is 'self-liquidating'. Normally proof of product purchase is required before the consumer can take advantage of such offers.

(vii) *Free mail-in.* This is similar to a free 'in/on/off-pack' offer except that the consumer is asked to send in for the give-away item, and some proof of previous product purchase may be required.

(viii) *Container premium.* In this case, the product is pre-packed in a container which can be used by the consumer, for example, instant coffee in a glass coffee pot. The public may or may not be required to contribute towards the cost of the container.

(ix) *Purchase privilege plan.* This applies when, on making a purchase of one product, the consumer becomes eligible to receive another at a specially reduced price.

4. *Merchandising and Point of Sale Material*
This category of below-the-line promotion includes display cards, dump bins, leaflets, showcards, and any other material

paid for by the manufacturer or retailer to encourage the consumer to make the transition from appraisal to purchase in the in-store situation.

5. *Sponsorship of Sporting and Other Events*
This usually takes the form of the manufacturer contributing in whole or in part to the cost of an event or its participants.

SELLING INTO THE PIPELINE

The offers made to channel intermediaries as an inducement to stock the manufacturer's product include:

(i) Cash discounts and increased margins.
(ii) Free goods, for example 13 for the price of 12.
(iii) Incentives in the form of competitions, free gifts, or dealer premiums such as trade self-liquidating offers.
(iv) Salesmen's incentive schemes.
(v) Exhibitions.
(vi) Insertions, for example leaflets inserted in trade magazines.
(vii) Direct mail shots, letters, or leaflets sent to the trade through the post.

The actual 'hardware' of promotion alone—the plastic daffodils, the more substantial gifts exchanged for trading stamps, and all the other goods that change hands in the form of a promotion—amount in value to £200m. a year, according to a recent estimate. This figure is made up as follows:

Retail value of goods supplied for cigarette coupons. £64m.
Combined retail level of values of trading stamps from the two major companies, Green Shield and Sperry and Hutchinson. £28m.
Goods offered as premium promotions. £102m.

Total: £194m.

Source: British Premium Manufacturers Association (1969).

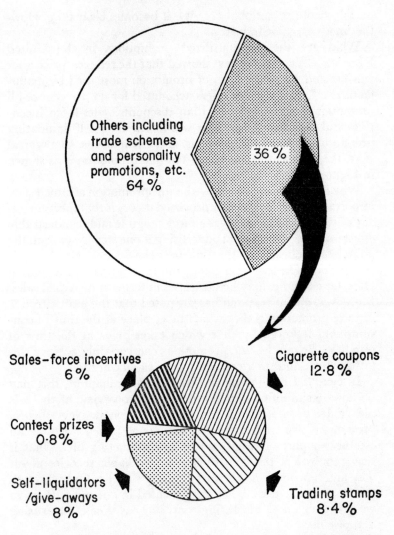

Figure 1.4. Merchandise expenditure by type of promotion (*Source: The Financial Times*, 7 November 1968)

Thus, when one adds in the sums spent on trade discounts (this is a cost, even if money does not change hands—it is an opportunity cost of profit foregone), the costs of products given free in samples, coupons, and extra-quantity deals and all the periphery of promotional activity, it becomes clear that below-the-line is a major industry.

What are the most utilized promotions in the United Kingdom? A recent survey[1] showed that the reduced price offer was far and away the form of promotion most used by manufacturers. Reduced price offers accounted for 30 per cent of all promotional activity other than discounts, sales-force incentives and merchandising. This was followed by self-liquidating premium offers, then by coupons, and free mail-ins. In a typical year, the expenditure on below-the-line promotion is as shown in Figure 1.4.

Why has this swing to below-the-line promotion assumed such importance? One frequently proposed theory is that the immediacy of such promotions gives a more tangible and demonstrable effect on sales. Traditional advertising is one step away from the point of purchase and the link between it and sales levels is contentious. On the other hand, the exact impact of a coupon offer, for example, may be measured in terms of increased sales. Moreover, recent research has suggested that the most effective form of promotion is that which takes place at the time of consumption, followed by that which takes place at the time of purchase. Below-the-line promotions can certainly achieve this latter effect, and, to a certain extent, the former too.

In fact, as I hope to demonstrate in later chapters, this may be an oversimplified and possibly dangerous view of the role played by promotions in the purchase process. Nevertheless, promotions are used and used extensively; they are now an established part of twentieth-century marketing life. What is now required is the construction of workable theories about why and how promotions work the way they do. Only through this approach can we be as sophisticated in our use of them as we are with other marketing tools such as theme advertising and pricing.

[1] M.S. Surveys, *Promotions '69*.

CHAPTER TWO

THE PROMOTIONAL
ENVIRONMENT

IF there have been dramatic changes in promotional activity in recent decades, then there have been even more dramatic changes in the nature of retail business. These changes in the structure of distribution have had ramifications for below-the-line activity and may, to a certain extent, have encouraged its growth in some ways whilst dampening it in others.

That the 'corner shop' is almost an historical phenomenon is an observable fact. So, too, is the growth in supermarkets; in 1960 there were 400, in 1970 there were 4,000. In the same way that the size of retail unit is increasing whilst their total number declines, so the percentage of business being done by the multiple stores is increasing. In 1960 multiples (chains with ten branches or more) had approximately 25 per cent of the grocery trade in the United Kingdom, in 1970 it was over 40 per cent, and most of this growth was at the expense of the independents. Figure 2.1 shows how multiples, with only a small percentage of the number of retail outlets, dominate the scene in terms of sterling business. There has also been a steep decline in the total number of retail establishments, the 1966 Census of Distribution showing a fall of $8\frac{1}{2}$ per cent over 1961. In grocery outlets, there was a more pronounced reduction in the number of outlets. Between 1961 and 1969 they are estimated to have declined by over 20 per cent.

Thus the picture that emerges seems to be one of fewer shops doing more of the total business. A result of this has been that whilst competition between stores may have declined, the competition between brands *within* the store is now so much greater. The greater range carried by the modern supermarket places the brand in a highly competitive environment. The housewife is surrounded by a bewildering array of cues, some overt and some tacit, urging her to choose one brand rather than another. Thus, the in-store impact of a promotion, particularly on impulse sales, can be highly important, in ways to be discussed later. At the same time that these basic changes in the nature of the retail scene have been occurring, there has been an accompanying change in the rate of product-innovation.

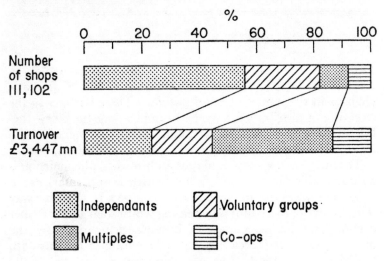

Figure 2.1. The grocery trade, 1969

PRODUCT-INNOVATION

One of the major features of the post-war retailing scene has been the increasing pace of new product development, particularly in groceries. Manufacturers have, by and large, adopted the philosophy that the key to modern marketing success lies in innovation and, at the same time, no longer supporting dying brands that cannot be resuscitated without large injections of financial support.

To put this in perspective a recent study[1] found that of 3,000 food products listed as new between 1959 and 1965, only 47 per cent were still in national distribution in August 1969. Frozen foods showed the biggest number of launches during the period at 516, followed by canned meats with 401 new-comers. Success rates were 37 per cent and 33 per cent respectively.

[1] *The Financial Times*, 8th April 1970.

Crisp bread, however, with only 14 new products, had a success rate of 90 per cent, and instant desserts with 26 introductions gained 89 per cent acceptance. Major companies better able to afford the heavy level of investment and continuous marketing back-up fared better than small ones.

Clearly therefore, the situation in the stores is now highly dynamic, as more and more brands jockey for a share of the housewife's purse. The high failure rates experienced in some markets make product-innovation a risky business, yet without innovation the modern company is unlikely to maintain its profit level.

As a result of this situation, below-the-line promotions have found a ready acceptance by the majority of manufacturers because of their ability to achieve an immediate impact in terms of short-term volume. If a new brand, recently launched, is fighting for consumer acceptance, then a promotion can be one more incentives to the shopper to cross the purchase threshold. A new brand always has the problem that it is an unknown quantity in the housewife's eyes. There must be good arguments in its favour before she can be persuaded to forsake her existing brand of which she has experience, for something about which she may know nothing. Obviously there can be many cues to help the purchaser over the initial threshold— the manufacturer's name, the interest, and possibly excitement generated by theme advertising and in-store merchandising— but below-the-line promotions, if carefully used, can be a major element in the adoption process.

Fewer outlets and more brands is thus the major retailing development over the last ten years, and it is therefore not surprising that the retail outlet takes on the appearance of a battleground with opposing brands locked in a struggle, the results of which may be measured in terms of pay-offs, or losses, of millions of pounds.

To confound and confuse the situation still further has come a phenomenon of some considerable importance; the 'private label' or 'own brand' product.

THE RISE OF THE 'PRIVATE LABEL'

The 'private label' has been present on the retail scene in one form or another for some time. By 'private label' or 'own brand' products we mean those products that are sold under a retail organization's house brand name and sold exclusively through that retail organization's outlets. These products are not necessarily manufactured and/or packaged by the retail organization, but may be made for them—often by a manufacturer whose major business is in selling the same product under *his own brand label*.

The following figures give some idea of the strength of the private label in various retail sectors at the time of writing:

1970 'Private label' market shares

By class of goods (%)

Packaged foods	13
Household goods	7
Toiletries and cosmetics	6½
Pharmaceuticals	4
Confectionery, nuts, crisps	4
Women's wear	20
Men's wear (excluding tailoring)	16

By type of store (%)

Grocery:

Multiples	12–14
Co-ops	9–11
Symbol Ind.	2–3
Other Ind.	—

Chemists:

Multiples	15–16
Independents	1–2

Source: Private Label Reviewed (J. W. Thompson Co. Ltd, 1970).

It can be seen therefore that in some retail sectors the private label has made a big impact. A further feature of the phenomenon is that in some cases private label accounts for as much as 40 per cent of a store's business, for example, Marks and Spencer, British Home Stores and Sainsbury, and in others it can be 20 per cent or more, for example, Tesco, Fine Fare, and Boots. A recent study[1] estimated that in the food markets private label accounted for an annual value of around £300m.

What is the distinguishing feature of the private label as against the branded product? It is quite certainly one thing—price. A recent study by Nielsen[2] covering 18 product cate-

[1] *Private Label Reviewed*, op. cit.   [2] *Nielsen Researcher*, July/August 1969.

gories in the grocery market indicated that the private label brands were between 10 per cent and 49 per cent cheaper than the national brands, with an average of around 24 per cent.

These dramatic price differences are achieved as a result of the minimal expenditure by the retail organization on promotional backing for these lines, either above or below-the-line. Whereas the national brands are supported by often quite massive marketing appropriations, the private label is able to achieve a very respectable share of the market without such support. It has been argued that in fact the private label is reaping the fruits of the national brands' promotional efforts, in that although they share in the demand created or maintained for the product generally, they do not share in the promotional costs involved in this creation and maintenance.

Whatever the rights and wrongs of the private label situation, it is a phenomenon that is probably here to stay. The circumstances in which the national manufacturer finds himself are problematic. Often the private label which is eroding his own market share is supplied by him in the first place—yet it represents such a slice of his own business that he would be loath to forgo it. Thus the branded goods manufacturer, unable to match the private label on its own terms, i.e. price, must necessarily devote even more expenditure to maintaining those aspects of the 'brand' that by the nature of branding are unique. In other words, the manufacturer needs to build in 'added values' which may or may not be tangible, and the only way in which these values can be emphasized and communicated to the buying public is via theme advertising.

Some manufacturers of branded products have attempted to counter the attraction of private labels by increasing below-the-line expenditure. To a certain extent there is a logic in this.

The 'excitement' and attraction of the private label is essentially an in-store phenomenon. The real battle in this case is taking place on the supermarket shelf. On the one hand is a nationally advertised brand, with its 'added values', and on the other hand, the private brand, an anonymous product, with a large price advantage. In this in-store situation, the added attraction of a suitable below-the-line promotion may just be sufficient to weigh the scales in favour of the national brand.

C

By and large, however, the increase in the strength of the 'private label' may militate against the increased use of below-the-line, particularly if this were to be at the expense of theme promotion. As will be demonstrated in later chapters, 'money off' is the most popular promotion of all with the housewife, and it is unlikely that the national brand can counter this attraction in its own below-the-line consumer promotion. It makes more sense, it would seem, to strengthen those attributes of the brand that the private label cannot claim, i.e. those intangible elements that constitute the 'personality' of the brand.

THE FIGHT FOR SHELF-SPACE

As the scale of the retail operation increases and as the pace of innovation steps up, a major determinant of a brand's success is the distribution that it achieves—distribution both in terms of the number of stockists and in terms of the amount of display it achieves within the outlet. In grocery retailing, the trend towards self-service has meant that the point-of-purchase is often the point-of-decision in terms of brand choice. In a busy supermarket, inches of shelf-facing can often be crucial—it has been suggested that the percentage share of sales for a product within a supermarket which a brand achieves will be roughly equal to the percentage of shelf-facing that it is given. That self-service has increased in retail outlets is self-evident. Figure 2.2 demonstrates the steady trend away from counter service in the grocery sector.

The manufacturer of the national brand is thus faced with a situation that is quite new: a multi-brand choice situation for the consumer with that choice arrayed before her face-to-face. Thus the growing importance of marketing activities designed to achieve an impact at the point of purchase, in particular merchandising and below-the-line promotion aimed at the consumer. But in addition to this important area there is a further facet to the problem already identified—that is actually to gain distribution in the store and, with it, achieve the best possible shelf-space.

It is in this crucial area that those types of below-the-line promotion which are aimed specifically at the retailer are relevant. These promotions may take the form of competitions for the retailer, premium promotions, gift offers, and so on. However, the major and most controversial form of dealer promotion is the discount. Discounting at the retail level can take several forms: generally it will be in the nature of a straight percentage reduction in price. Sometimes the arrangement will be more complex, with discounts being negotiated in return for specific shelf-space allocation or as a 'fee' for carrying an in-

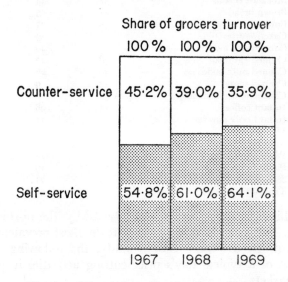

Figure 2.2. The trend to self-service (*Source*: Nielsen)

store promotion. With the growth in retail buying power, examined in more detail below, the extraction of discount has become, in many markets, a prerequisite for any distribution at all. If these discounts represent a charge on the marketing budget, as they usually do, then the manufacturer has less to spend on maintaining the brand's values and personality through theme advertising. The implications of such a situation will be examined in later chapters.

In an attempt to gain attention at the point of purchase, the manufacturer must constantly compete with his rivals for the installation of display material and special displays of his brand. A study by Gallup[1] showed the extent to which grocery super-

---

[1] *Gallup Shopping Basket*, 1968.

markets were carrying display materials for brands in certain product areas.

All stores	Display materials including special displays of brand	
	In shop (%)	In window (%)
Breakfast cereals	51	44
Brown bread	21	5
Butter	40	27
Cakes/pastries	58	9
Canned dog foods	52	20
Canned cat foods	48	20
Canned milk puddings	36	26
Canned soups	44	9
Chocolate confectionery	41	6
Instant coffee	41	28
Instant milk powder	20	11
Margarine	34	10
Meat and vegetable extract	50	26
Paper handkerchiefs	43	14
Paper kitchen towels	30	9
Soft toilet tissue rolls	54	27
Tea (not tea bags)	62	36

To this bewildering jungle must be added the in-store promotion. These can be of all types, but the most prevalent is the price cut. In the same Gallup study, the following picture emerged of a typical day's price-cutting activities in grocery supermarkets.

All stores	Manufacturer's price cuts (%)	Store price cuts (%)
Breakfast cereals	7	28
Butter	—	15
Cakes	18	11
Canned dog foods	42	26
Canned cat foods	28	22
Canned milk puddings	—	18
Canned soups	—	16
Chocolate confectionery	15	8
Instant coffee	11	22
Instant milk powder	28	9
Margarine	24	13
Meat and vegetable extract	58	12
Paper handkerchiefs	16	16
Soft toilet tissue rolls	—	22
Tea (not tea bags)	8	42

All this concentration on in-store activities by the manufacturer presupposes that there is a high element of impulse purchasing on the part of the consumer, and that he or she does not always plan her *brand* choice in advance, and that he or she may alter a planned choice when presented with certain stimuli in the purchasing situation.

A study by Simmons[1] divided grocery expenditure into four categories:

(1) *Specifically planned*: product and brand known before the shopper arrived at the store.
(2) *Substituted*: specifically planned, but brand substituted in the store.
(3) *Generally planned*: product, but not brand, known before shopper arrived at the store.

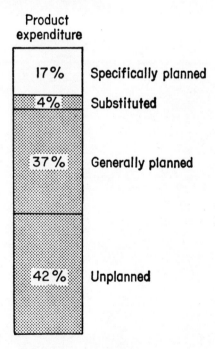

Figure 2.3

[1] Simmons, M., 'Probing the Point of Sale', paper delivered to seminar sponsored by The Incorporated Society of British Advertisers, and the Association of Market Survey Organizations, November 1968.

(4) *Unplanned*: shopper had no intention of buying the product when arriving at the store.

Over a broad range of product categories, the percentages in Figure 2.3 emerged from the study. More specifically, the pattern of impulse buying shown in Figure 2.4 emerged. There can be no doubt, therefore, of the importance of in-store factors such as shelf-space and display in enabling manufacturers to capitalize on the impulse purchase. The problem lies in the fact that this capitalization can often only be achieved through excessive discounting and thus at the expense of above-the-line expenditure.

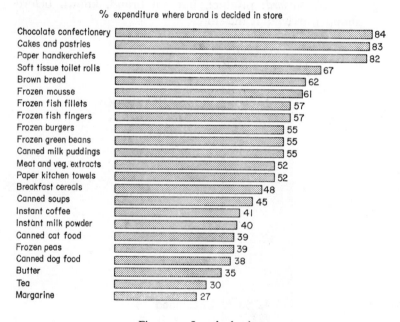

% expenditure where brand is decided in store

Product	%
Chocolate confectionery	84
Cakes and pastries	83
Paper handkerchiefs	82
Soft tissue toilet rolls	67
Brown bread	62
Frozen mousse	61
Frozen fish fillets	57
Frozen fish fingers	57
Frozen burgers	55
Frozen green beans	55
Canned milk puddings	55
Meat and veg. extracts	52
Paper kitchen towels	52
Breakfast cereals	48
Canned soups	45
Instant coffee	41
Instant milk powder	40
Canned cat food	39
Frozen peas	39
Canned dog food	38
Butter	35
Tea	30
Margarine	27

Figure 2.4. Impulse buying

MANUFACTURER, RETAILER, CUSTOMER: THE ETERNAL TRIANGLE

Considerable attention is currently being given to the growing power of the retailer and the implications that this holds for the marketing environment generally. Of greatest importance to the promotional planner is the degree of influence that the retail sector is able to exert over promotions. In many cases, a promotion will only be accepted by one of the larger supermarket chains if the chain determines the timing, and suitable discount terms are available. Often, too, the *type* of promotion will be influenced by the retailer's attitude. The 'in-store give-away' promotion has been effectively quashed by the retailer's reluctance to handle the administration of it. The growth in power of the large multiple in the marketing channel is largely a function of their purchasing power. In 1969 multiples did £1,400m. of business, and £1,000m. of this was accounted for by the ten biggest groups. Obviously the manufacturer who is faced with this sort of customer is not in a strong position to dictate its in-store marketing policy.

This shift in the locus of power in the marketing channel may be ascribed to several movements. J. K. Galbraith[1] has suggested that where one channel unit becomes of such a size that it is the effective source of power in the channel it will eventually be countered by the actions of those who are subjected to this power. In other words, 'private economic power is held in check by the countervailing power of those who are subject to it'. Thus the once-dominant manufacturer has been displaced by the very force that it generated—mass marketing. The logic of large markets and of the huge investments in stocks required to present the large choice of products and brands to the consumer has inevitably resulted in a larger retail unit. At the same time there has been a movement amongst the smaller units to group together in voluntary schemes to make purchases in bulk, for example, Spar and Mace in the U.K. grocery field. Nielsen[2] has shown that in 1969, 746 trade buying points covered 77 per cent of the grocery business. This figure of 746 was made up as follows: 430 Co-operative Societies in Great Britain (this figure is declining considerably as retail societies merge and as more central buying is done by the C.W.S.); 203 head offices of multiples, including their subsidiaries; and 113 wholesalers serving the symbol independents (voluntary trading groups). The picture is clearly one of fewer

[1] Galbraith, J. K., *American Capitalism* (Houghton Mifflin, New York, 1957).
[2] *Nielsen Researcher*, March/April 1970.

purchasers accounting for a growing percentage of retail business.

In a situation such as this, there are few options available to the manufacturer. Perhaps one of the most viable strategies is one which runs counter to the present trend towards more expenditure below-the-line. It can be argued that the only way out of this impasse is for the manufacturer to establish a *direct franchise* with the consumer. This franchise would be in the form of an increase in consumer brand loyalty; a situation in which, because the brand has so many 'added values' as well as its intrinsic product qualities, the consumer will always demand that brand and thus serve to 'pull' it through the marketing channel, rather than the present situation in which the brand is often having to be 'pushed' through the channel by means of discounts and other trading incentives. Such a strategy of brand value-building requires a major investment in theme and corporate advertising. This conflict between the requirements of value-building and point of purchase impact is a theme to which we shall return in later chapters.

RETAILERS' ATTITUDES TO BELOW-THE-LINE

The central role of the retailer in the manufacturer-retailer-consumer triangle requires that some attention be given to their attitudes to below-the-line promotions generally. What sort of factors impinge on their willingness to carry a promotion, and what do they think are the most effective types of promotion for generating sales volume? Several surveys have attempted to answer these questions, and one of the most extensive was that carried out amongst 423 retail outlets in the Bradford/Horniblow, Cox-Freeman study of below-the-line promotion.

In this study retailers were asked first to indicate the influence which specific factors had on their attitude towards promotions generally (see questionnaire in Appendix B). An analysis of their replies in relation to two specific product fields, toothpaste and instant coffee, yielded the following results (there were no significant differences between replies for the two product classes):

Overall Ranking of the Influence on Retailer Attitude towards Promotions for Toothpaste and Instant Coffee

(1)   Product is a brand leader.

(2)   The power of the promotion to attract customers into the store.

(3)   The extent to which the brand is advertised on TV.

(4)   Amount of above-the-line advertising planned to back the promotion.

(5)   Value of the promotion to the consumer.

(6)   Rate of stock-turn of product.

(7)   Percentage retail market.

(8)   { Frequency of use of promotions by brand manufacturer.
       { Amount of in-store display offered with promotions.

(9)   Amount of space taken by promotion and product.

(10)   Offers currently running on other brands.

(11)   { Amount of time taken up by the promotion.
       { Amount of inconvenience caused by the promotion.

(12)   Existence of own brand labels.

These preferences held across all demographic and retail classifications.

Thus it would appear that the three most important factors in gaining dealer acceptance of a consumer promotion are that the product should be a brand leader, and that the promotion has a drawing power of its own, and, importantly in view of present trends, that the brand be advertised on TV. Those factors taken least into account appear to be: promotional activity of competitive brands; the amount of time and inconvenience caused by the promotion; and the existence of a 'private label'.

The results of the questions aimed at producing a ranking of those promotions perceived to be most effective in generating sales volume are shown below. Again there were no major differences between the rankings produced for toothpaste and for instant coffee.

Overall Ranking of Effectiveness of Promotions on Sales

(1)   Money-off to consumers.

(2)   Coupons to consumers.

(3)   Extra quantity in packets.

(4)   Gift on packs to consumer.

(5)   On-pack offer of discount on next purchase.

(6)   { Money back on proof of purchase.
         On-pack coupons towards next purchase.
         In-store demonstrations/sampling.

(7)   Gift at check-out to consumer.

(8)   { Dealer cash discount.
         Free sample to consumers.
         Free gifts on proof of purchase.

(9)   Re-usable containers (not applicable to toothpaste).

(10)   Quantity discount to dealers.

(11)   Personality promotions.

(12)   { Dealer competition.
         Premium promotion.

(13)   Consumer competition.

The results showed no significant differences across demographic or retail classifications. The remarkable feature of this ranking is that it matches, to a large extent, consumer preferences as reported in Chapter 6.

A similar study carried out by Marketing Advisory Services showed a very similar ranking in terms of perceived affect on sales:

(1) Manufacturer's price cut.
(2) Temporary increase in pack size.
(3) Coupons representing money discount to consumers.
(4) Free gifts with packs.
(5) Trading stamps.
(6) Premium promotion.

In this chapter we have identified several major areas of change in a promotional environment. This is the background against which present-day promotional activity should be viewed. To a certain extent, much of the growth in below-the-line expenditure may be attributed to these changes. In the following chapters, attempts will be made to develop the rationale of below-the-line from something more than a hasty reaction to a changed competitive environment (which in many cases it has been) to an element in a considered, integrated corporate communications mix.

CHAPTER THREE

THE CORPORATE ROLE OF BELOW-THE-LINE

BELOW-THE-LINE promotion is just one vehicle amongst several available to the brand manager to enable him to meet his marketing objectives. Promotion is in fact an element of the company's 'marketing mix'. By marketing mix, we mean quite simply that collection of tactical and strategic devices that comes under the domain of marketing—for example, the price of the product, its package, its channel of distribution, the advertising theme, and so on. To a greater or lesser extent these elements are variable and may be combined in such a way as to produce different results in terms of sales, or whatever the yardstick of success in the company is.

The skilful brand manager will attempt to experiment with various combinations of the total mix in an attempt to optimize the sales or profit situation for the brand. Some of the elements in the mix may be relatively fixed—the channel of distribution, for example—whilst others such as promotion may be highly variable. A feature of below-the-line promotion is that it is essentially a short-term weapon (even though, as we shall examine in later chapters, it may have long-term effects). The brand manager may hurriedly introduce a promotion to bolster a sagging sales graph, or he may wish to do something to counter a competitive marketing action. Below-the-line promotion has a major advantage in that it is flexible and can usually be introduced into the market place in a relatively short time. It is also something of a blunt instrument in that it is generally aimed broadscale across the total market and relies on a shot-gun effect for increasing consumer offtake. It does not yet have the same degree of fine tuning enabling it to be aimed at specific market segments that theme advertising has. Similarly, the brand manager generally has little research-based knowledge of the potential effect of this particular marketing weapon. Clearly, therefore, the specific role of below-the-line needs to be clearly defined in any marketing campaign.

It was suggested in Chapter Two that promotions could have varying effects in encouraging consumer acceptance and adoption of products. Everett Rogers[1] has postulated that the process of product adoption has five basic stages:

(1) *Awareness*: the individual becomes aware of the product but lacks information about it.
(2) *Interest*: the individual is stimulated to seek information about the product.
(3) *Evaluation*: the individual considers whether it would make sense to try the product.
(4) *Trial*: the individual tries the product on a small scale to improve his estimate of its worth to him.
(5) *Adoption*: the individual decides to make full and regular use of the product.

If we accept this framework as a starting point for our analysis, it is possible to suggest at which of these stages above- and below-the-line promotion may be of maximum effectiveness.

Theme advertising is more likely to be of considerable importance in achieving stages (1) and (2), and also (3). It is at stage (3) that below-the-line promotion may begin to hold promise. The potential consumer has already had his interest aroused in the product, and the fact that there is, for example, an offer of a price cut, may prompt the potential customer to move to stage (4), i.e. trial. A major incentive to this 'trial' may come through the medium of below-the-line, for example, a free sample or a coupon offer, enabling the consumer to purchase the goods at a much-reduced price, or trial can be achieved through free samples of the product. By the time stage (5) is reached, above-the-line advertising comes back into its own in reinforcing the consumer in her belief that she has made the right decision in purchasing the product and in encouraging repeat purchase. Repeat purchase can also be stimulated by certain types of below-the-line promotion, for example an offer which requires the collection of packet tops.

[1] Rogers, Everett, *Diffusion of Innovations* (Free Press, 1962).

The length of time that the product has been on the market will also have implications for the brand manager. There is a soundly based theory that all products have 'life cycles', that is, they move through quite clearly defined stages in terms of their sales volume. Figure 3.1 illustrates the stages in the sales of a typical branded product.

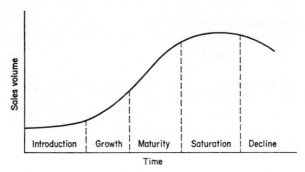

Figure 3.1. Product life cycle

Kotler[1] has listed five stages in this cycle:

(1) *Introduction*: the product is put on the market, awareness and acceptance are minimal.
(2) *Growth*: the product begins to make rapid sales gains because of the cumulative effects of introductory promotions, distribution, and word-of-mouth influence.
(3) *Maturity*: sales growth continues, but at a declining rate because of the diminishing number of potential customers who remain unaware of the product or who have taken no action.
(4) *Saturation*: sales reach and remain on a plateau marked by the level of replacement demand.
(5) *Decline*: sales begin to diminish absolutely as the product is gradually edged out by better products or substitutes.

Below-the-line promotions can often be of considerable importance in a brand's introductory phase in helping the product to achieve an initial high level of penetration. Similarly, below-the-line promotions can often be used to halt the decline

[1] Kotler, P., *Marketing Management* (Prentice Hall, New Jersey, 1967).

of a product, at least temporarily, and to maintain its sales peak or even to put it higher by encouraging new consumers to try the product.

The twin concepts of the adoption process and of the product life cycle can be of great use to marketing management in ensuring that the greatest effect is achieved from a particular promotion.

Sampson and Hooper[1] provide a useful summary of possible marketing objectives and how they may be achieved by specific below-the-line promotions:

Marketing objectives	*Promotional type*
(1) Consumer trial—new users	(a) Product or sample distribution
	(b) Coupon distribution
	(c) Off-label deals
	(d) Banded packs
(2) Repeat purchase	(a) Reduced price pack
	(b) Buy one, get one free—alternatively, price refunded
	(c) Coupon on first pack
(3) Display—prime shelf position	(a) On-pack premium
	(b) Banded pack—related item
	(c) Mail-in premium
	(d) Consumer competition
	(e) Window display competition
(4) Defence against competition	(a) Reduced price pack
	(b) Twin pack—same product
	(c) Banded pack—related items
	(d) Premiums—on-pack
	(e) Competitions
(5) Distribution	(a) Sample distribution to consumer
	(b) Coupon distribution to consumer
	(c) Dealer loader (discount)
	(d) Trade competition
	(e) Salesmen's incentives

This check-list provides only a generalized summary, and each marketing problem will call for its own specific solution.

LONG-TERM VERSUS SHORT-TERM

It is apparent that some marketing problems are of a short-term nature whilst others are essentially long-term. By 'short'

[1] Sampson, P., and Hooper, B., *Thomson Silver Medal Paper* (Thomson Organisation, London, 1970).

and 'long' term, we refer not to specific periods of time but rather to the type of problem encountered. For example, sales of a brand may suddenly fall, and upon examination the fall is attributed to a promotion being run by a competitor. If sales may be expected to recover after the impact of the promotion has declined, then this would be a short-term fluctuation. On the other hand, the success of the competitor's promotion may be such that it has permanently induced some of our customers to switch brands. In this latter case, we may find that the fall in our sales, unless countered by increased marketing effort on our part may assume some permanence, i.e. the problem becomes long-term.

Traditionally, it is assumed that below-the-line promotions are a short-term tactical weapon suitable for the solution of short-term problems. Thus, in the example quoted earlier, where our sales have been eroded as a result of a competitor's promotional activity, we could counter this by mounting a promotion of our own which would, hopefully, restore the *status quo*: or even perhaps increase our sales over their original level. This sort of close-quarter fighting is a phenomenon of the present promotional scene. The two major United Kingdom petrol companies, Shell and Esso, have engaged with each other on several occasions in recent years in promotional battles in order to secure a short-term advantage.

The problem is, of course, that promotions used in this way tend only to be short-lasting palliatives for use in a fire-fighting situation. A more satisfactory role for below-the-line promotion would be as a part of a concerted, integrated promotional effort to achieve long-term brand objectives. This approach requires a greater act of faith and patience than would be the case if promotions were used conventionally.

A crucial consideration, but one that is rarely taken into account in promotional planning, is the long-term effect on the brand of a series of promotions. This problem is considered in some depth in Chapter Seven, and suffice it to say here that the possible detrimental long-term effects of a series of promotions could be such as to outweigh any short-term advantages resulting from their indiscriminate use.

The measurement of the effectiveness of a promotion is a topic to be discussed later, but it is instructive to consider the broad parameters that measure success over time. In Figure 3.2 a typical sales curve is illustrated, showing the change in retail offtake before, during, and after a consumer promotion. The short-term success of the promotion may be measured, in crude sales terms, by the difference between A and B, and the cost involved in achieving this difference.

The medium-term success of the promotion would be measured over a number of buying cycles to determine if

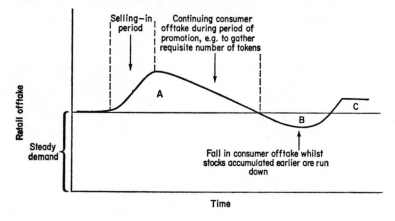

Figure 3.2

repeat purchase by customers who were drawn to the brand by the promotion is being achieved. This is represented in the figure by area C, i.e. the increase in the level of steady demand.

The long-term success of a promotion is something far more intangible to assess. Essentially, and this is a theme to which we shall come back repeatedly, the long-term effect must be measured in terms of whether the brand suffers through a devaluation of its 'image' and 'value' in the consumers' eyes through the repeated use of below-the-line.

PROMOTIONS IN THE CORPORATE CONTEXT: U.K. RESEARCH FINDINGS

As part of the study of the whole phenomenon of below-the-line promotion in the United Kingdom sponsored by Horniblow, Cox-Freeman Limited, a small-scale study of fifteen United

Kingdom consumer marketing companies was carried out in June 1970. In each company, contact was made with the personnel most intimately concerned with below-the-line promotions and their attitudes to specific aspects of the phenomenon were probed by means of an open-ended questionnaire (see Appendix C). A remarkable degree of agreement on the questions was found between companies, and the investigators felt confident in drawing the following conclusions.

Involvement in Below-the-line
All the companies interviewed in the study were engaged in below-the-line promotion to a greater or lesser extent. The number of national promotions engaged in during the twelve months prior to the interview ranged from four to one hundred and twenty, with a median of thirty-five. Several companies recorded a very large number of localized or specific store promotions; on one case a thousand such exercises were estimated for the previous twelve months.

At the outset, the respondents were asked what the concept of below-the-line meant to their companies. The majority defined it as being any promotion other than media/theme advertising, and a good number also included merchandising and salesmen's incentives in their definition, although there were as many companies not including incentives in their definition. One company saw the concept in broader terms as being 'a short-term tactical measure to generate profitable incremental sales volume', whilst another defined below-the-line as being 'everything that does not tell the housewife something about the product'.

Some companies had a remarkable history of activity below-the-line. Several companies quoted instances of free gift promotions in the mid-nineteenth century, although most of the activity seems to have started after World War I, with a spate of competition-type promotions. More recently, however (mid-1950s onwards), the increase in promotional activity has been phenomenal. Respondents were asked what type of promotion their companies had used over the last three years, and in fact the question would have been better phrased by asking them what types had they *not* used. The only type of promotion that seemed to be little used was the 'personality promotion', and more recently there seems to be a growing dissatisfaction with competitions. The general picture seemed to be that whilst there was often intense promotional activity it was generally on tried and tested promotional schemes, and that new developments in promotional activity were not forthcoming.

Reasons for Involvement with Below-the-line

Companies were questioned on the reasoning behind their involvement in below-the-line activities, and, not surprisingly, a wide diversity of reasons were advanced. One company reported that in some instances they used below-the-line aggressively to expand a market, but more often they were forced to use it defensively—to hang on to what they had. The reply that occurred most often was that it could be used to support a brand by encouraging or maintaining brand loyalty. It had the added attraction to several companies in that it seemed to be a direct way of influencing sales. One company saw below-the-line as a tactical marketing weapon, as a 'fast corrective to competitive pressure'. Many companies described below-the-line as fulfilling specific objectives, for example, to promote display, to motivate salesmen, to get an interested audience with the store manager, and generally to add interest to the brand in the in-store situation. Surprisingly, a sizeable number of companies felt that they used below-the-line simply, as one put it, 'because it's there', and that there was no clearly thought-out underlying ideology for the use of below-the-line in these companies.

The Role of Below-the-line in the Company's Marketing Effort

Respondents were asked whether they viewed above- and below-the-line promotions as substitutes for one another, and if not, how were they able to offer something distinct. The majority of companies did not view above- and below-the-line as being substitutes but rather as being complementary to each other. The general feeling seemed to be that above-the-line promotion developed the brand image, whilst below-the-line had a more supportive/tactical role in the total promotional programme. It was felt that these two forms of promotion had different objectives; below-the-line is (1) competitive, (2) a tool for gaining distribution and display, (3) an attempt to create volume at the point of sale; whereas above-the-line builds a customer franchise, and, hopefully, would reduce the need for below-the-line.

Above-the-line promotion represented to many respondents a long-term device with long-term pay-offs, whilst below-the-line, if it were to have a pay-off, would be essentially short-term. One company thought that in some instances above- and below-the-line could be substituted, but in only one way, i.e. substituting above for below. For example, trial purchase could be achieved by exclusive use of above-the-line promotion.

There was a fair degree of agreement that different types of below-the-line promotion would have different effects in the market place. The most commonly stated effects were:

Bargain pack	Increases loyalty amongst existing users.
Trade bonuses	Attain distribution.
Self-liquidators	Create in-store interest.
Collecting packet tops	Encourages repeat purchase.
In-pack offers	Encourages trial.

One company felt that there were distinct market segments for promotion—for example, age groups—and their policy was to attempt to match a promotion to the segment. It was generally felt that the choice of promotion was dependent on the marketing objectives for the product.

Respondents were asked if their companies used below-the-line in a defensive manner. The majority of companies had used below-the-line in this way, some on occasions, others more regularly. The consensus of opinion seemed to be that a certain amount of promotion has to be defensive with an established product to maintain market share. Specific reasons given for using below-the-line defensively were: in a situation where the product was suffering from a price disparity with private labels; or sometimes used to 'load' the trade to keep down competitive products; or to make new entry difficult for would-be competitors.

Objectives and Evaluation of Promotions
There seemed to be a widespread attempt to formulate specific

marketing objectives for below-the-line promotions amongst the companies interviewed. Objectives stated ranged from the straightforward 'to increase volume' to the more sophisticated approach adopted by one profit-centre organized company who placed specific contribution requirements on a promotion. Amongst the most common objectives given were:

To increase market share.
To support a flagging product.
To motivate salesmen and to improve distribution.

Most companies applying clear objectives to their promotional activity used these objectives as a yardstick against which to measure the achievement of the activity. Little use was made of redemption rates as a measure of success, the feeling being that these did not really reflect anything meaningful. One company derived information from its regular consumer diary, and the same organization also cross-checked the effect of promotional activity on its weekly image/advertising survey.

There were some differences between the companies interviewed in their approaches to the pre-testing of below-the-line promotions. Most companies attempted, or had attempted, some kind of test, although few were confident of their worth. The most common form of pre-testing was to use the subjective judgement of the marketing team! One company tried the promotional concept out on its secretaries before going ahead and developing it. Several companies had tried user-tests and store-tests and one company, using theatre tests, reported 'incredibly close' predictions of the success of the promotion. The major value of testing to these companies seemed to be in terms of choosing between promotional alternatives rather than in using the results to make estimates of their effectiveness.

Management of Below-the-line
The crucial question of how to split the total promotional budget between above- and below-the-line is one to which the companies had obviously given some thought. In only a few cases were rough rules of thumb used, such as 'it depends how many promotions the product can bear in a year', and 'we

stick to a fairly constant percentage'. The majority of companies reported that their decisions were made in the light of pre-determined marketing objectives. For example, one company sets volume objectives at the beginning of the year, and then estimates how much needs to be spent to achieve these objectives. Another company viewed the problem in terms of 'how much emphasis do we want to give to short-term promotion as against long-term?'

The actual decision on what form and type of promotion was generally left to the brand or product manager with responsibility for the product. Most companies, if they had a promotions manager, expected the decision to be very much a joint one. Only one company reported that it took its advertising agency's advice on what form of promotion to run.

Most companies had a fairly heavy dependence on specialist promotion agencies to handle the execution of the promotion, and in some cases these agencies devised the form of promotion (for example, they may prepare a competition for the company, and run the whole thing on their behalf).

There seemed to be a general wariness on the part of the people interviewed on relying too heavily on specialist agencies to provide objective information about below-the-line promotions generally. The sort of service that is expected from a traditional advertising agency—for example, attitude surveys, image checks, attempts at measuring effectiveness and so on—are not looked for in the promotion agency. Most companies rely on their salesmen, the trade press, and their own awareness to supply them with information of competitive industry. Nielsen, A.G.B. and Attwoods were all named as sources for providing information on volume and distribution. The overall impression was summed up in one statement: 'Every promotion is unique at a specific point in time, so information tends to be of a general nature and of little permanent use.'

The Influence of the Retailer

Respondents were asked what influence the retailer had on the pattern of below-the-line activity in which they engaged. The consensus was that the retailer was indeed a force to be reckoned with in the plotting of below-the-line promotional strategy. The feeling was that the larger retailers were becoming much more demanding about promotions in terms of frequency, timing, and the terms they were offered. Instances were quoted where retail chains had effectively stopped the use of in-store give-aways. There seemed to be a wide experience of the larger chains 'charging' the manufacturer to run a promotion. It seems clear that these larger chains are having a definite effect on the type of promotion being run. Not surprisingly, most companies questioned were unhappy with this state of affairs, and their feeling was summed up by one respondent: 'There is a need to strengthen customer franchise so that the retailer's power is reduced.' Nevertheless, the recognition of this growing retail power has led many of the companies interviewed to 'tailor-make' promotions for the larger retail companies.

When questioned on the need for increased promotional activity in the face of a decline of the 'brand', approximately half the companies felt that the brand was still very much alive, and that in only a few fields were brands becoming mere 'commodities'. On the other hand, one company thought that too much indiscriminate below-the-line activity could in fact weaken the brand differential, and lead to a commodity-type situation. Similarly, respondents did not think that the growth in private brands would lead to a greater need for below-the-line activity. It was generally agreed that the way to combat private labels was through greater use of above-the-line promotions. This was, it was felt, because private brands sell on price alone. Theme advertising can offer some differential other than price.

Generally speaking, the changing structure of the retail scene did not seem to be changing the need for greater or less below-the-line promotion. Where it was having an effect was in the loss of manufacturers' power to have complete discretion on when and where to have any form of promotion.

CHAPTER FOUR

PROMOTIONS AND THE
PROMOTIONAL MIX

IN many ways the biggest problem with below-the-line promotion lies in reconciling its effects with those of theme advertising. Each type of promotion has, as we have seen, specific effects, below-the-line being generally short-term in terms of sales effects and above-the-line generally long-term. Yet in a sense the purpose of the two is ultimately to produce a particular sales level or some other marketing objective. Perhaps by separating the two we are forcing an artificial dichotomy, and we may, as a result, be operating dysfunctionally in that the effect of sales promotions, when seen as an end in themselves, may be at variance with the desired effect of the product's theme advertising. For example, as we shall examine in a later chapter, an unsuitable promotion could have a catastrophic effect on a carefully devised theme programme in terms of attitudes towards the product and the image of the product and the company.

Many of these problems can be avoided by attempting to construct an *integrated* promotional plan where both above- and below-the-line are used as complements to each other, rather than as unconnected elements in the marketing mix. With the advent and acceptance of corporate planning and the total approach to the company's activities that this requires, there has been a movement towards the integration of sub-systems within the total system, i.e. the company and its markets. Such an integration requires the correct identification of the interrelationships and interfaces that exist between such sub-systems. So it should be with the promotional sub-system, involving as it does considerations of corporate image, brand image, and the whole tool-bag of promotional techniques that are available to influence them.

We may identify three major advantages accruing to the company from an integration of its promotional activities. These are:

Joint effects, the possibilities for 'synergy'.
A reinforcement of the brand's 'message'.
A reduction of contradictions in the promotional plan.

Joint Effects

Reference is frequently made in business planning to the 'two plus two equals five' effect. Expressed more simply, this is the effect that is achieved when the whole is greater than the sum of the parts. In plotting strategies for diversification the corporate planner, under this scheme of things, would attempt to select those products or markets which tied in neatly with his existing products or markets in such a way that either savings could be made through the use of joint facilities or revenue increased by having a complemented product line.

Ansoff[1] has defined this effect as 'synergy', and describes how marketing synergy can occur:

> Synergy occurs . . . when products use common distribution channels, common sales administration, or common warehousing. Opportunities for tie-in sales offered by a complete line of related products increases the productivity of the sales force. Common advertising, sales promotion, past reputation, can all have multiple returns for the same dollar spent.

It is with the possibilities for synergy in sales promotion that we are concerned here. By attempting to make the relationship between above- and below-the-line 'synergetic' we are in effect trying to get more mileage from the same promotional pound. We could imagine, for instance, a situation where the M.G.C. Company was considering a sales promotion in order to counter a cyclical dip in consumer offtake. Traditionally in the company the choice of the promotion would have been left to the Promotions Manager, who, working within his annual budget, would have done his best to achieve this particular sales objective. On the other hand, the advertising agency

---

[1] Ansoff, H. I., *Corporate Strategy* (McGraw-Hill, New York, 1965).

handling M.G.C.'s theme advertising, although vaguely aware of the coming promotion, have had their copy platform and their media schedule worked out well in advance, and see no reason to change. Thus two separate departments, Sales Promotion and the Agency, are working hard within their separate budgets to maximize their own separate objectives. Yet in a sense the long-run sales objective of the company and the objectives of the two arms of the company's promotional effort coincide. M.G.C. may well be able to meet this long-run objective more efficiently by using above- and below-the-line promotion not as separate tools but as adjuncts to each other. For example, M.G.C., wishing to counter the cyclical dip in sales, could well combine theme and promotion, using perhaps the creative experience of the agency, in a single campaign at a combined cost less than the two originally separate campaigns. When we discuss the measurement of promotional cost effectiveness (Chapter Seven) we shall be concerned with the assessment of this type of effect both in terms of the reduced cost and the increased impact.

Reinforcing the Brand's Message
Increasing the impact of the company's total promotional effort by using linked below-the-line promotion is a joint effect. Advertising a gravy-boat which can be bought at a reduced price with two gravy packet tops is an example of how the relative impact of the two forms of promotion may be enhanced. But more than this, the promotion, if carefully devised, can strengthen and reinforce the message of the brand advertising. If the message of the theme promotion is that giving the family gravy with their meal is being a good mother and wife and that gravy has connotations of goodness and homeliness, then something which could be useful in the family situation would make a suitable premium promotion. The gravy-boat would encourage usage of the product in the first instance and further, when seen on the table, could invoke the scenes of domestic bliss presented in the theme advertising.

This scenario is by no means atypical, and experience is showing that this approach where theme and promotion are creatively linked can have such a reinforcing effect.

On the other hand, the wrong promotion can have the reverse effect. In Chapter Seven we discuss the effect on the long-term 'saleability' of the product of a series of short-term promotions. In a different way a promotion can lead to negative synergy by being totally unsuited to the product and its market. The offer of a promotion which is perceived by the consumer to be cheap and nasty and/or irrelevant can undo a favourable effect created by theme advertising. If an integration of promotional advertising is necessary, it is equally necessary to ensure that the promotion fits the product and the potential purchaser. There must be many a brand manager with a warehouse full of household rubber gloves and steak knives following an inappropriate promotion! There is also the possibility that, as well as being left with a lot of merchandise, he has also damaged the brand-image by having the promotion in the first place.

Reducing Contradictions in the Promotional Plan
To a large extent, this third benefit from an integrated approach is managerial. Under separate management there is a higher degree of risk that the left hand of advertising will not know what the right hand of promotion is doing.

Some of the possible conflicts have been examined above. In addition to these problems, however, there is likely to be no co-ordination in terms of timing, target audience identification, and promotional objectives if the two are kept separate. In essence, promotion, be it above- or below-the-line, is there to perform a particular role in achieving marketing objectives. It makes no sense from a strategic point of view to separate the two. They are both part of a total corporate communications effort and sensibly they should be the responsibility of the same department. More than this, though, they should not be seen as being separate tools but rather as complementary devices for achieving a particular goal or set of goals.

Creatively, too, there will be benefits from integrating the promotional effort. A first-class below-the-line programme in its own right might not make much sense in terms of the sustained theme advertising programme current at the time of the promotion if it is designed and executed independently.

Many of the foregoing comments are commonsense, yet few companies in the author's experience have adopted such an integrated approach to promotional planning. In an attempt to counter this, the remainder of this chapter is devoted to possible strategies for making this suggested approach operational.

PROMOTIONS AND THE PRODUCT PLAN

The product plan is the axis around which, in the modern company, most marketing effort revolves. The product plan (or marketing plan), as a planning document, should ideally begin with a statement of marketing objectives and then describe the strategy whereby these objectives may be achieved. Within the plan will be co-ordinated all the various elements of the marketing mix at the product manager's disposal. Financial budgets and targets will also be included.

Promotion, as an element in the marketing mix, should figure prominently in the product plan. There will obviously be a statement of the budget available for promotion but, further than this, there is a requirement that promotional objectives be laid down and that the specific promotional vehicles that are to be used to meet these requirements be defined. The sophisticated product planner will require criteria for evaluating the success or otherwise of his product strategy; similarly he should attempt to provide a means of measuring the effect of promotional activity.

Barnes, McDonald and Tuck[1] have suggested a classification of objectives and measurement criteria for below-the-line promotions:

Objectives	Success criteria
(1) To gain consumer trial for a new brand.	Number of promoted units taken up. Number of new users who repeat purchase. Profit per promoted unit and profit for those unpromoted units which can be ascribed to the promotion.
(2) To reactivate interest in a flagging brand.	Ascribable profit from both new and former users who take up the promotion. Effects on attitudes.

[1] Barnes, M., McDonald, C., and Tuck, R., *Thomson Silver Medal Paper* (Thomson Organisation, London, 1970)

Objectives	Success criteria
(3) To stimulate off-season interest.	Ascribable sales and profits against promotional costs.
(4) To secure good distribution and display.	Distribution and display increases. Increases in impulse buying, shop turnover, trade goodwill.

This classification is not necessarily complete, and specific promotions may have highly particular purposes. Nevertheless, whatever the objectives of the promotion, some measuring rod will have to be devised to check its efficiency. The more precisely the promotional objectives are stated, the easier will be the evaluation. The problem of evaluation will be dealt with in a later chapter, but it will be clear that the major problem lies in interpreting just what effect is due to the promotion and what would have happened anyway. Thus we need to find some method of ascribing additions to profit which result from the promotion. Similarly, we need to discover means of measuring the *long-run* effect on a brand of a sustained series of promotions.

The classification above relates only to the operational objectives of a promotion. In addition, we must be concerned with questions of fitting the promotion within the broader objectives. Here we get back to the 'reinforcement' aspect of promotional activity. The brand objectives should override such considerations as short-term sales headaches, if, by curing these, we are going to work against the longer-term brand objectives. There is an obvious point of conflict here which can only be reduced by adopting an integrated approach to promotional planning. If above- and below-the-line are in the hands of separate departments then the conflict is likely to be exacerbated.

Examples of such long-term brand objectives for a food product could be: to increase a market share by at least 4 per cent a year over the next five years; to trade the product up from its present C2, D segment to include C1 customers; to establish the product as a wholesome yet inexpensive food item. Every product in a company's product line should have such clearly stated and accepted objectives. Given this basis, promotional planning has a higher chance of achieving an optimum mix between all forms of promotion available to the company.

BUDGETING FOR BELOW-THE-LINE

The question of how much to spend below-the-line is a crucial one. The Bradford/H.C.F. survey found a variety of methods in use amongst the companies surveyed. The majority of companies reported that their decision was made in the light of pre-determined marketing objectives. For example, one company set volume objectives at the beginning of the year, and then estimated how much needed to be spent to achieve these objectives. Another company viewed the problem in terms of 'how much emphasis do we want to give to short-term promotion as against long-term?' The less sophisticated marketing companies tended to use rules of thumb, such as 'it depends how many promotions the product can bear in a year', or 'we stick to a fairly constant percentage below-the-line'.

The danger of rules of thumb such as the two just quoted lies in the fact that promotional objectives are not formulated, or, if formulated, are ignored. Using a constant percentage has the same attendant dangers as setting advertising budgets using a percentage of last year's sales revenue. Thus if sales were down last year, advertising will be down this year—having the effect, in many cases, of accentuating the downwards sales spiral.

The integrated approach to promotional planning would suggest that a more satisfactory form of budgeting for below-the-line could be achieved not by attempting to make a split in the total promotional budget, and saying 'x per cent below-the-line, y per cent above' but rather by using an objectives-oriented approach.

An example of this approach is that suggested by Morgan:[1]

(a) Determine, in order of priority, the problems facing the brand.
(b) Determine the money available to solve the problems.
(c) List and cost all the possible alternative solutions to the problems, e.g. theme advertising, consumer promotions, pricing strategy, product change, etc.
(d) Estimate (or guestimate) the effectiveness of each solution.
(e) If the answers to (c) and (d) suggest that a promotion is the

[1] Morgan, Ann, *A Guide to Consumer Promotions* (Ogilvy & Mather, New York, 1970).

most efficient answer to the brand's problem, and if the answer to (b) shows there is enough money for a successful promotion, then a promotion is indicated.

This scheme requires that, given a total promotional budget (to cover all forms of promotion), we look at each marketing problem, decide how much money we have available to solve it, and then see which promotional activity (above, below, or both) can do the job best within the budget constraint.

This approach has the merit of being simple. In practice, there are further considerations. We must always use the *net* cost of promotion (be it above- or below-the-line). In other words, we are interested in the addition to revenue accruing through sales of the product, the cost of the promotion, any receipts to offset these costs (e.g. as with premium promotions of the self-liquidating type) and, most importantly, the effect of the promotion on long-run saleability. It is now clear that what is required is an elaborate costing procedure in order to complete stage (c) in the check-list above.[1]

MONITORING PROMOTIONAL PERFORMANCE

It has been emphasized that a prime reason for defining promotional objectives is to provide a yardstick for measuring promotional performance. This is not so difficult as far as the measurement of short-term effects are concerned (such as the change in consumer offtake), but problems arise when long-term effects are being assessed. The aim of a specific promotion could be to improve distribution in particular outlets, and the method used may be some form of discount to these dealers. The immediate impact of this can be very quickly detected in terms of increased offtake by the dealers, but there may be a longer-term effect in that the dealers may pressurize for similar discounts on all future sales. The only means of controlling this situation would be via an increased and strengthened franchise with the consumer. This can only be established by more and better theme advertising (assuming that the product variables

[1] One approach here could be the use of an objectives-oriented budgeting system such as that provided by output budgeting (see Christopher, M.G., Walters, D. and Walb, G.S.C. *Output Budgeting in Marketing*, Management Decision Monograph, 1972.)

are satisfactory). There are also problems of separating the effects of above- and below-the-line promotion (see Chapter Eight).

Nevertheless, it is essential that we have a regular system for monitoring the effect and effectiveness of our promotional effort. How are attitudes towards our brand changing as a result of promotions? To answer this, we need a regular check on attitudes. We need also to relate this information to the propensity to buy the product. How much more or less likely is the consumer to purchase our product following this particular promotion? Continuous attitude testing of this sort would not be cheap, but it would provide a Distant Early Warning System which would indicate that things were or were not happening as they should be. When compared with the possible long-term danger to the brand's profitability, this type of control is money well spent.

The information that the monitoring system needs to provide would typically be:

Brand share and trend.
Marginal contribution to profits and increased sales.
Competitive action/reaction.
Attitude changes on relevant dimensions, e.g. brand 'personality', perceived utility of brand, specific product attributes.
Changes in propensity to buy.

Given this sort of information, it should be possible to check the performance of the *total* promotional effort. When it comes to investigating below-the-line promotion's contribution, the conclusions will inevitably be based more on intuitive judgement than on science. Nevertheless it is imperative that this sort of analysis be carried out and the results acted upon if promotional effectiveness is to be maximized.

Figure 4.1 illustrates how an operations, planning and control cycle for integrated promotional planning can be constructed. This type of sequential framework offers a means of extracting the maximal sales value from a promotional pound, whilst at the same time ensuring that the possible long-term dangers from below-the-line are minimized.

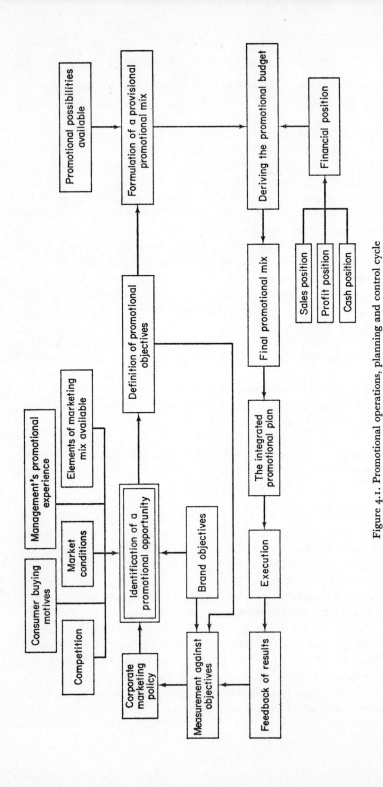

Figure 4.1. Promotional operations, planning and control cycle

CHAPTER FIVE

THE BEHAVIOURAL CONTEXT OF PROMOTIONAL ACTIVITY

THE COMMUNICATIONS PROCESS
Only connect . . . (E. M. Forster, *Howards End*)

THE study of effects as they relate to media and their various messages is a favourite area for the advertising researcher. The problem with effects is that they are often very difficult to allocate to a cause. The problem is enhanced by the traditional reliance of marketing researchers on the handy, but dangerous, stimulus-response (S-R) paradigm which, in the case of advertising and promotion, sees purchase (the response) occurring as a direct effect of these stimuli. In reality, the situation is far more complex; a whole array of stimuli interact, in many dimensions, to produce differential responses. Instead of a straight linear relationship, i.e. A causes B, we have a multidimensional matrix, impossible to interpret by existing methods of analysis. Systems analysis with its total approach and awareness of interconnections could possibly provide such a framework for analysis.

The concern in this book, however, is not with the analysis of the marketing communications process but with a specific vehicle within it. Nevertheless, an appreciation of the totality of communication is necessary if below-the-line promotions are to be seen in their proper perspective. In later chapters, we shall be concerned with the interconnections between below-the-line and other communications vehicles as they impinge on the total process. Similarly too, effects are dynamic; they do not stand still in immutable relationships for all time—they change frequently, sometimes predictably, often not. Thus we need to be aware of the longer-term effects of a communications programme.

Communications theory is a rich and expanding science. It offers the marketer a means to a greater understanding of how all types of promotion work, simultaneously providing the basis for making existing communications more effective.

Essentially, the generalized model of the communications process views the system in terms of messages transmitted by the seller, in a language chosen hopefully to be understood by the target audience, to the potential consumer, who interprets the message and perhaps acts upon it (Figure 5.1).

The message is transmitted via a communications channel or

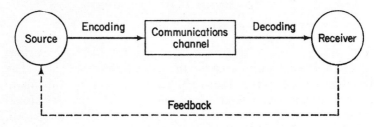

Figure 5.1

channels, which could take the form of personal communication, TV advertising, a free sample through the letterbox, or via any of a hundred other possible channels. Communication occurs when information is passed and received. Thus information about a product can come from usage or from display on a supermarket shelf as well as via the media of print and the screen. We therefore need to take a wider view of communication, one that incorporates the information content of the product, and its related peripherals (for example the package). Extending this idea, it can be seen that information can flow through various channels in different ways. Conventionally, a distinction is made between *horizontal* and *vertical* channels of communication. Horizontal channels are those that exist between members of one level in a marketing hierarchy, for example one housewife talking to another. Vertical channels, as the name suggests, exist where information flows from one level to another, for example from the manufacturer to the consumer via a TV commercial. We may, therefore, extend somewhat our original simplified view of the marketing communications process (Figure 5.2).

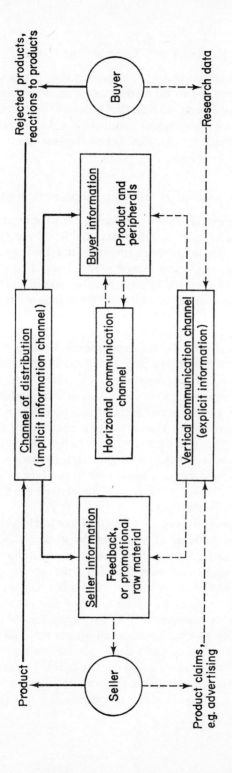

Figure 5·2

(After: Kernan, J., Dommermuth, W. and Sommers, M., *Promotion: An Introductory Analysis*, McGraw Hill, 1970.) Reprinted with permission.

The important point to grasp here is that the product itself and its peripherals can be a communications vehicle, and that the channel through which the product is distributed can double as a communications channel. It is in this context that we shall attempt to examine below-the-line promotion as a communications vehicle.

STIMULUS-RESPONSE IN THE MARKETING PROCESS

The experiments of Pavlov in which he produced measured conditioned reflexes in animals have achieved a certain notoriety, and the implications of his and later findings have long been accepted by the marketing practitioner. However, whilst in the strictly controlled laboratory situation it was possible to determine with some exactitude the response to particular stimuli this is clearly not the case in the marketing process. In an environment in which there are many competing stimuli in the form of a multitude of communications, with a high level of noise and where there is a great variability amongst the perceived needs of the consumer, it is clear that the simple stimulus-response mechanism is not a realistic model of market response. It is therefore not sufficient to postulate a direct link between a promotional stimulus and a response in the form of purchase. Rather, it is necessary to consider the consumer as a complex of motives, beliefs, attitudes, desires, and so on, which interact upon the receipt of a stimulus to produce a behavioural response. This 'black box' of the consumer's psyche may be represented as in Figure 5.3.

The concept of intervening variables is central to a fuller understanding of the response of consumers to promotional stimuli. It explains why different consumers will react in different ways to the same stimulus. A money-off offer may be acted upon by some in the form of increased purchases because they perceive the offer to be a bargain, whilst to others the same promotion may represent a 'cheapening' of that brand's value to them.

Similarly, the motivation of the consumer will differ considerably from individual to individual. Motivation may be defined as 'behaviour that is instigated by needs within the individual and is directed towards goals that can satisfy these needs.'[1]

[1] Morgan, C. T., *Introduction to Psychology* (McGraw-Hill, New York, 1956).

Motives are very much the impetus to behaviour. A need is perceived by the individual, producing a drive to achieve a goal (need-satisfaction) through the act of purchase and consumption. There have been various classifications of 'needs', generally in the form of hierarchy in which certain needs have to be fulfilled before others, this hierarchy being a function of

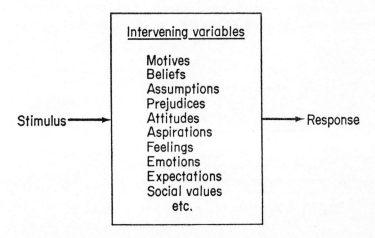

Figure 5.3. 'Black box' of consumer's psyche.
(After Pratt, R. W., 'Consumer Behaviour—Some Psychological Aspects', in G. Schwartz (ed.), *Science in Marketing*, Wiley, New York, 1965).

the 'life style' of the consumer. Life style may be defined as:[1]

> ... The distinctive or characteristic mode of living, in its aggregative and broadest sense, of a whole society or segment thereof. It is concerned with those unique ingredients or qualities which describe the style of life of some culture or group, and distinguish it from others. It embodies the patterns that develop and emerge from the dynamics of living in a society.

There is one further element in the marketing process to complete this behavioural framework. This is the concept of

[1] Lazer, W., 'Life Style Concepts and Marketing', in *Toward Scientific Marketing*; S. A. Greyser (ed.), Proceedings of the Winter Conference of the American Marketing Association, 1964.

'learning'. Learning occurs through experience and exposure to situations. In the marketing process, this will generally occur through purchase and consumption. Experience is clearly capable of producing change in consumer behaviour, be it in the form of strengthening or weakening brand loyalty, or in the form of future participation or non-participation in

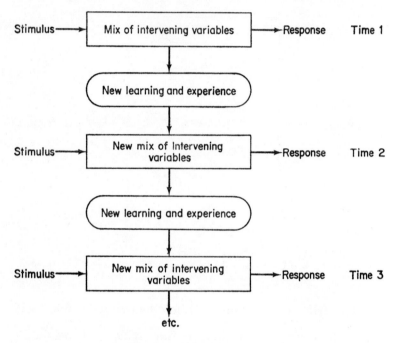

Figure 5.4 (After Pratt, *op. cit.*)

particular promotions. An extensive body of theory has grown up around the role of learning in the marketing process and experimental data demonstrates its importance in the purchase sequence. Bringing these strands together, we can postulate a dynamic paradigm of the consumption process (Figure 5.4).

In this model the consumer is undergoing a constant change in terms of the interactions within the 'black box' which may well produce differential responses over time to the same stimuli. Similarly, at one period in time, the same stimulus will produce different responses between different consumers. These differences are due to basic differences in the consumers' cognitive processes, i.e. the mechanisms of the black boxes.

How does this affect the manager involved with below-the-line promotion? This can best be answered by considering the promotion as a communications vehicle. Communication is the major influence the company can bring to bear on the learning and cognitive processes of the consumer. All communications emanating from the company, be they through the media or in the form of below-the-line promotion, are a direct inter-personal link with the consumer. They are a spur to involvement by the consumer with the company's product and a continuous reinforcement to repeat purchase. Later in this chapter special attention is given to the problem of involvement and partici-pation by the consumer in the purchasing sequence. Essentially, however, the promotional manager is attempting to encourage *commitment*, and this involves the identification of the behavioural dimensions of the market. In addition to this, it is not sufficient to examine the results of a promotion simply in terms of how many people were motivated by the promotion but also in terms of *who* was motivated by it. Consumer reaction to pro-motional efforts cannot be assessed therefore solely in terms of sales: account must be taken of the effect on attitudes, on beliefs, and all the other intervening variables relevant to the situation. When market segmentation is discussed in Chapter Six the differential behavioural make-up of different market groups emerges as a criterion for promotional segmentation.

ATTITUDES AND ATTITUDE-CHANGE

The role of 'attitude' figures prominently in the contemporary marketing man's paradigm of the consumption process, and indeed the role of attitude can be central to many marketing situations. We may define an attitude as:[1]

> ... A mental and neural state of readiness, organised through experience, exerting a directive of dynamic influence upon the individual's response to all objects and situations with which it is related.

[1] Allport, G. W., *Handbook of Social Psychology*, C. Murchison (ed.) (Clark University Press, 1935).

Three basic components to attitudes may be identified: an evaluative, cognitive element, embodying a 'belief' about the object under study: a 'feeling' component, describing the emotive aspects of the object; and an 'action tendency' component, describing behavioural intentions. 'Attitude' may be seen, therefore, as being somewhat more complex than appears at first sight. Its importance to marketing derives from its centrality in the buyer behaviour process. There is considerable evidence to suggest that attitudes determine behaviour, given the presence of a motivational force. Thus attitudes towards the product are a major determinant of purchase.

Attitudes are formed and changed to a large extent by exposure to information which may be acquired through consumption or through communication. Furthermore, the nature of an attitude is dynamic in that it can change considerably over time; similarly attitudes, either positive or negative, may be reinforced over time.

The problem for the marketing manager is to identify the salient attitudes involved in the decision to purchase his product. In addition, he must know what forces may alter these attitudes, and, in this context, what effect below-the-line promotions may have upon attitudes towards the product and how attitudes towards below-the-line affect participation in the promotion. These are crucial requirements for a fuller understanding of the effect of promotions upon the long-term image of the brand.

In the example below, typical attitude configurations are given which illustrate how attitudes towards the promotion may affect attitudes towards the product. In this example, attitudes are looked at in terms of their three basic components.

Typical Attitude Structures to a given Promotional Situation

	Favourable configuration	*Unfavourable configuration*
	Towards the promotion	
Cognitive component	I believe the promotion offers good value for money.	These promotions are a waste of money.
Feeling component	I am in favour of cheap offers.	They should reduce the price instead.
Action-tendency component	I will participate in the promotion.	I won't participate in the promotion.

Towards the product given the promotion

Cognitive component	This brand often gives me a bonus in the form of a promotion.	This brand is having to give bribes in order to sell it.
Feeling component	This brand is generous, it is friendly.	It must not be selling very well, I suspect that its quality is low.
Action-tendency component	I will buy the brand again.	I won't buy it.

It is often said that the role of corporate communications is to affect a positive shift in consumers' attitudes towards the company's products. If this view is accepted, it must also be accepted that inappropriate communications may have the reverse effect. How might the effect of a promotion upon an attitude be measured? Various methods exist, but a typical format could be the 'before and after' approach, where consumers' attitudes to the product in question are examined in terms of the basic components, defined above, before the launch of a promotion, and then measured again after some duration of time. Assuming that the correct experimental procedure is employed, and the scales used in the test are appropriate and pure (i.e. do actually measure what they purport to measure), this approach can be a quick and cheap monitor of the effect of promotions upon attitudes towards the product.

Of some relevance at this juncture is the theory propounded by Fishbein.[1] Fishbein, an American psychologist, has postulated that an important determinant of behaviour is the attitude held by the subject towards the *act* of behaviour as well as the attitude towards the *object* of the behaviour itself. In other words, in a given situation, the attitude towards the act of purchase must be examined as well as the consumer's attitude to the actual product. Recent findings seem to bear out this duality as a determinant of purchasing behaviour. Its implications for marketing men may be profound in that it introduces a hitherto unidentified element in the pre-purchase sequence. For below-the-line promotions, it suggests that the attitude held by the consumer towards the *act of participating in the promotion* must be considered to be of equal importance as the attitude held towards the promotion itself. Thus, the key to promotional success may

[1] Fishbein, M., 'Attitude and the Prediction of Behaviour', in *Readings in Attitude Theory and Measurement*, M. Fishbein (ed.) (Wiley, New York, 1967).

well lie in many instances, in a favourable disposition by the target group to participation in the specific promotion under consideration. Put this way, it has the ring of commonsense, but the major pay-off of the Fishbein model is that the procedure involved in quantifying these elements of attitude and relating them to behaviour is relatively straight-forward.

Little research has been reported that attempts to evaluate below-the-line promotions in terms of their effect on consumer actions from a behavioural point of view. If we accept a major role of marketing management to be 'the construction of a theory about a market' it becomes necessary to break way from the 'black box' approach to promotional planning, which merely attempts to maximize output from a given input, and move towards an understanding of the inner mechanisms of the process. In this way, the promotional planner is better able to exploit the potential of below-the-line.

RECENT RESEARCH INTO CUSTOMER ATTITUDES TO BELOW-THE-LINE

The majority of published research on consumer attitudes to below-the-line has tended to be highly qualitative in nature and has generally examined users' verbalizations of their *feelings* towards below-the-line. In a major work,[1] Schlackman examined the statements of a small sample of housewives concerning below-the-line promotion. From these statements, Schlackman postulated that, in the case of price cuts, there was 'an indication that housewives acted in such a way as to routinize and normalize their shopping behaviour'. In other words, the housewife was rationalizing the observed price cuts in such a way that it would fit her already preconceived purchasing framework. Thus, if the price cut was on a brand towards which the housewife was already favourably disposed, she would rationalize the price cut by suggesting that the cut, if made by a supermarket, was made possible by a large turnover, or, if made by the manufacturer, by the competitive nature of the market. These price cuts were thus not seen by the housewife with favourable predispositions as representing a sacrifice in quality.

[1] Schlackman, W., 'Some Psychological Aspects of Dealing', in *Research in Marketing* (Market Research Society, London, 1964).

On the other hand, if the brand was untried or little known, then the price cuts took on much more of a quality-related meaning: 'I don't mind a price cut if it's on a brand I know, but I wouldn't be so sure if it was a brand I hadn't tried. I would think, well, perhaps its cheap and not so good.'

There were indications, too, that where price cuts were becoming prevalent that the housewife was losing all conception of the 'normal' price for the product, and therefore the impact of a price cut was being diminished.

The premium promotion evoked a mixed response from the housewives questioned, but it generally appeared to be the case that there was a more ready acceptance of this type of promotion when the article being offered in the promotion clearly represented value for money. Free gifts, such as a banded pack, were typically perceived to be useless and of poor quality and, in some instances, it appeared to reflect unfavourably upon the manufacturer and the product.

In the Bradford/Horniblow, Cox-Freeman study of 1,000 United Kingdom housewives some interesting unprompted statements in evaluatory terms emerged. These are summarized in Table 5.1.

The theme that seems to recur throughout these statements is the perception of the value of a promotion by the respondents. It tends to suggest that the likelihood of a more favourable disposition towards the act of participating in the promotion (in Fishbeinian terms) is enhanced when the perception of value is high.

There is clearly a need for basic research into the role of a company's promotional activity in bringing about attitude-change and/or reinforcement. For every promotional project it becomes necessary to pre-test at least in terms of simple attitude checks. The nature of the promotion, too, must be assessed in terms of consumers' evaluatory perceptions. Having this information at his finger-tips provides the promotional planner with a surer basis for action.

INVOLVEMENT AND PARTICIPATION

It has been suggested elsewhere by this writer[1] that certain

[1] Christopher, M. G., '2001: The Existential Consumer', in *British Journal of Marketing* (Autumn 1970).

TABLE 5.1. *Unprompted Statements by Housewives*
(*Source*: Bradford/H.C.F. Study.)

Favourable comments	(%)
Think promotions are a good idea/they should have more	10
Like money-off offers, but others just put up prices	8
Like free samples/free samples give you a chance to try new products	6
Think coupons are a good idea/make you buy new products	4
Some are all right, but others aren't	4
Promotions are good to introduce new products	3
Lots of goods offered are very good value	1
Other favourable comments	6

Unfavourable comments	(%)
Prefer to have prices reduced instead of promotions	31
Don't like any of these promotions	10
Don't like coupons/coupons are just a nuisance/tend to forget coupons	5
Want more value for money, not free gifts/want value for money	5
Don't care much for competitions	3
Most of the free gifts are just rubbish	3
Money spent on promotions means an increase in price of product	2
Never know if there is a catch when they say '3d off'	1
The free samples are good quality, but when you buy the product, the quality is not so good	*
Other unfavourable comments	4

No comment	11

* less than 0·5%

subtle, yet pervasive changes are occurring in the nature of consumer behaviour generally. These changes, which are manifested in patterns of purchasing behaviour, are the result of a basic underlying mutation in the attitudes and perceptions of the consumer towards products. These changes are reflected in the approach employed by the consumer to his problem-solving behaviour. The concept of the 'problem-solving' consumer is relatively new. It suggests that the consumer, particularly when he is contemplating a purchase involving some 'risk' (economic or social), will approach the purchase decision in the ways he might solve any other problem. The consumer will therefore utilize all available 'cues' relating to the purchase decision. These cues will typically involve the product-related aspects such as price and product attributes, but also the information afforded by advertising and promotions may be regarded as a cue. In other words, everything that tells the consumer something about the product may be utilized in solving the purchase problem. Trends in consumer behaviour tend to suggest that the customer is becoming more 'involved' in the purchasing process. By this we mean that no longer is a bag of flour purchased, but instead a 'bundle of values and attributes' in the form of a bag of flour is being bought. In a sense too, the purchasing process undertaken by the housewife becomes an extension of herself; the contents of the shopping bag tend to reflect the personality of the customer and, more than this, the housewife regards the choice of products bought as being the most sensible disbursement of her funds to solve the weekly shopping problems. The problem of brand choice is central to the overall problem, and the conscious attempt by the housewife to discriminate between brands has implications for the promotional planner.

Thus there are two key emerging strands in contemporary purchasing behaviour: a higher degree of 'participation' in the sense of heightened problem-solving behaviour, and a greater involvement with the products themselves.

Under this analysis, we may see the typical promotion as filling two roles: first as a cue in that it carries information which may or may not be meaningful in the context of the purchase decision; secondly, the type of promotion may appeal to the particular personality of the buyer and participation in the promotion will say something about the housewife herself. Taking this point of view, the promotion can be much more than its innate qualities suggest, and indeed there is great scope for the *creative* use of promotions that fulfil these identified roles in such a way that short-term purchase and long-term image values are enhanced.

The framework suggested in this chapter provides a background against which consumer behaviour in relation to below-the-line promotion may be assessed. Only by understanding the behavioural environment of this particular consumer activity can we proceed to construct coherent and contradiction-free promotional strategies. Later chapters will present operational procedures in some depth, but the foundation for their successful implementation lies in a fuller understanding of the behavioural make-up of the particular marketing situation.

CHAPTER SIX

MARKET SEGMENTATION ANALYSIS AND PROMOTIONS

THE search for marketing strategies which will enable the firm to identify and capture discrete segments of the total market is becoming increasingly important. It is no longer sufficient or indeed practicable to appeal to the global market; there has been a recognition that markets are not homogeneous but rather are composed of several or many sub-markets. Each of these sub-markets or 'segments' represent a distinct and different grouping of consumers. This is not to say that the same product cannot be offered, undifferentiated, to more than one market, although this may be the case, but that the promotion of the product should be differentiated segment by segment. The concept of market segmentation is not new. Wendell Smith,[1] in one of the first presentations of the idea, suggested that:

> In the language of economics segmentation is *disaggregative* in its effects, and tends to bring about the recognition of several demand schedules, where only one was recognised before.

The implication of this concept is that different groups of consumers within a total market will react in different ways to a promotion. For example, the offer of a money-off promotion may increase demand amongst one group, whilst only having a slight effect on the other. The differential in response is accounted for in terms of the differences in the elasticity of the respective demand schedules.

Elasticity in this context refers to the response of demand to a change in the causal variable, in this case price. Figure 6.1(a) depicts the demand schedule for Market segment A of a

---

[1] Smith, Wendell, 'Product Differentiation and Market Segmentation as Alternative Marketing Strategies', in *Journal of Marketing* (July 1956), Vol. 21, No. 1.

company's market for its product and Figure 6.1(b) the demand schedule for Market segment B.

The implication for cost effective promotional management is clear: why not limit the promotion to segment A, or, preferably, use marginal analysis to promote to both segments differently, so that the marginal return to the promotion expressed in cost/benefit terms is the same? Strategies such as this call for a more creative approach to promotional design, the problem being

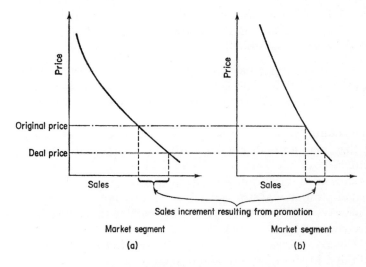

Figure 6.1

to identify and separate, for communication purposes, the market segments relevant to the profit/market situation.

Segmentation technology has become increasingly sophisticated in recent years. The search for criteria by which to segment markets has been accompanied by a growing armoury of procedures for obtaining such a segmentation. Criteria suggested have ranged from complex psychological discriminants to straightforward demographic criteria such as age, marital status, and so on. Attempts have also been made to segment markets on the basis of multiple criteria. Whatever the basis for segmentation, the result of a segmentation analysis should be the identification of groupings of customers who are more like each other within the group on all the dimensions relevant to the particular analysis than they are to members of other groups. In other words, segmentation analysis should aim at minimizing within-group variance and maximizing between-group variance. The achievement of such a state is a function of:

(1) Selecting those criteria that are relevant to the product and the promotion:

and

(2) Devising a means whereby, on the basis of the criteria stated in (1) above, natural segments within the market may be identified.

It has been suggested that some market segments may be more 'deal-prone' than others, or more specifically, certain promotions will have different effects amongst those segments. Given that this is so, present marketing tendencies towards blanketing the country with a national promotion, aimed at consumers as if they were a homogeneous market, are surely wasteful. If the intention of the promotion is to pull in the non-user of the brand, or to encourage light users to buy more, an undifferentiated promotional strategy will mean that the brand-loyal and the heavy purchasers will have a 'free ride' in the sense that they are covered by the promotion too.

Clearly, therefore, the marketing executive should be aware of the existence of differential response to promotional expenditure within a given market if he is to use below-the-line more finely as a marketing tool.

CRITERIA FOR SEGMENTATION

The choice of criteria whereby markets may be segmented depends on a number of important considerations:

(1) *The product/market situation*: segmentation must take into account dimensions that are relevant to the product and the market. In other words, steps must be taken to identify the product-related aspects of consumption behaviour as well as market features.

(2) *Operational viability*: markets should be segmented in ways that enable specific marketing action to be taken. This is

particularly important when attempts are made to create multi-dimensional segments.

(3) *Data requirements*: whilst a particular criterion may be highly salient to the product/market situation and be operationally viable, it may not always be possible to collect sufficiently accurate information to enable an effective segmentation study to be performed.

Traditionally, it has been usual for markets to be segmented along demographic lines. The problem here is that usually demographic features on their own do not adequately account for all the variance in buying behaviour. On the other hand, more sophisticated criteria, such as psychological dimensions, when used on their own, have similar shortcomings. The conventional market survey will usually confine itself to analysing the data by age, social class, area, and heavy and light usage. Only rarely, however, does a single criteria correlate well with purchasing behaviour, and indeed this matches modern thinking on consumer behaviour, which views the consumer as being influenced by his attitude to the product, his personal life style and social characteristics, his level of discretionary income, and so on. It is all these dimensions acting in concert that produce the final purchase. Meaningful segmentation must therefore reflect this multi-dimensional process by analysing markets according to all relevant criteria rather than one.

DEMOGRAPHIC SEGMENTATION

Demographic information, relating to age, sex, location, socio-economic class, and so on, can often provide a useful background to a segmentation study. On its own, however, the fact that product-usage is different in terms of volume between age groups tells the investigator little about 'why' it should be so. If promotional strategy is to make use of segmentation within a market there needs to be a behavioural statement about the phenomenon. Nevertheless, certain leads can often be found in an examination of demographic data. If a particular promotion has more success amongst one age group than another, this information will be of some use in the planning of a differentiated marketing strategy.

F

SEGMENTATION BY USAGE

It is often of value to know who the heavy and light users of a product are; it may be possible, for example, to generalize about the characteristics of the different groups and their response to promotional effort. The problems with usage characteristics are that they refer to past behaviour, and there is no guarantee that the characteristics of heavy users in the past will continue unchanged. Nevertheless, usage analysis is simple to perform, and can often provide a useful first step in identifying meaningful segments for promotional purposes. The mechanics of this analysis are simplified by using the techniques developed by Belson.[1]

An example of the procedure is given below in Figure 6.2. A sample of 1,000 housewives is questioned as to their usage of Brand X. The first step in the segmentation analysis is to determine a hierarchy of criteria whereby successive dichotomies of the sample may be made. At each dichotomy, the criterion with the best discriminatory power is selected.

In this example, three criteria are tested initially; social class, age, and household income. The sample is dichotomized by these criteria, and the heavy users in each group noted, there being 150 of the 1,000 who were classified as heavy users of Brand X.

The measure of discriminatory power that each criterion has is easy to compute; it is simply the difference between the proportion of heavy users that we might have expected to find in a resulting group, and the number actually found in that group (ignoring the sign).

Thus in this example, the discriminatory power (D) of social class is given by:

$$D = 50 - \left(\frac{150}{1,000} \times 400 \right)$$
$$= 10 \qquad \text{(sign ignored)}$$

Similarly, for 'age of housewife':

$$D = 70 - (0 \cdot 15 \times 700)$$
$$= 35 \qquad \text{(sign ignored)}$$

---

[1] Belson, W., 'Matching and Prediction on the Principle of Biological Classification', in *Applied Statistics*, Vol. 8, pp. 65–75.

(1) *Social class*
   (A,B,C1) and (C2, D,E)

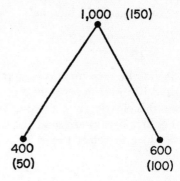

(2) *Age of housewife*
   (less than 35) and
   (35 and over)

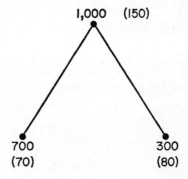

(3) *Household income*
   (less than £1,500 p.a.)
   and (greater than
   £1,500 p.a.)

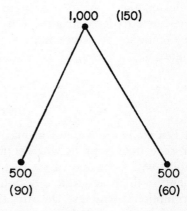

Figure 6.2. Usage analysis

and for 'household income':

$$D = 90 - (0.15 \times 500)$$
$$= 15 \qquad \text{(sign ignored)}$$

It may be seen therefore, that the first dichotomy of the data should be made according to the criterion of 'age of housewife', since this clearly gives a better discrimination of product-usage.

Further breaks are made in the data at each stage using this procedure to select the most powerful criterion. Eventually a

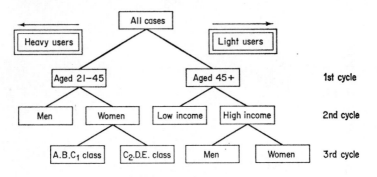

Figure 6.3. Usage segmentation

state is reached where either the resultant groups are too small to permit further meaningful dichotomies, or criteria no longer have sufficient disciminatory power. This method obviously relies on the prior identification of criteria before the survey questionnaire is constructed, but it is often possible to produce a segmentation structure akin to the hypothetical example in Figure 6.3.

SEGMENTATION BY ATTITUDINAL/PSYCHOLOGICAL DATA

It is a contentious point in marketing as to whether attitudes precede behaviour or whether attitudes change over time to adjust with behaviour. Both theories have equally strong arguments in their favour, and both have different ramifications for promotional strategy. Do attitudes towards promotions affect the ultimate purchase behaviour, or does purchase behaviour influence attitudes towards specific promotional activities? Either way, there are problems associated with using attitudinal and related psychological criteria in the segmentation study. The problems are of two types; identification of the dimensions (attitudes) and the measurement of them. Again the need is for the identification of salient attitudinal dimensions that reflect the product/market situation. One tried and tested method for deriving such salient dimensions is Kelly's Repertory Grid. The mechanics in this procedure have been elaborated in detail elsewhere,[1] but essentially the purpose of the Grid is to derive from a representative sample of respondents a battery of 'constructs' or bipolar dimensions which represent their personal evaluative framework in the purchase situation. To make this more clear: the use of this technique enables the investigator to bring to light a number of constructs relating to a product group such as expensive/cheap, long-lasting/short-lived, elderly image/youthful image, and so on. These constructs may then be used as the basis for the construction of a set of attitude scales.

Such a set of attitude scales could form the basis for a segmentation study and provide a means for a segmentation in terms of the consumers' perception of the competing brands in the market, and their relationship spatially. The problem at this stage is the concurrent analysis of a large number of attitude scores; for example, the respondents may have been asked to rate the brands in a market on 16 attitude scales, and the problem is to group the brands according to their received scores on *all* the dimensions simultaneously.

A technique which has been used successfully to overcome this problem is cluster analysis. Cluster analysis is a method of numerical taxonomy that examines a population simultaneously on any number of dimensions and observes how individuals within the population group or 'cluster' together. A simple two-dimensional example is shown in Figure 6.4, where each point represents a brand.

Clearly there are two major groups of brands. Now these groupings may or may not be different in terms of clearly separate consumer types. To make the analysis more realistic, a

[1] Bannister, D., 'A New Theory of Personality', in *New Horizons in Psychology*, B. M. Foss (ed.) (Penguin, Harmondsworth, 1966).

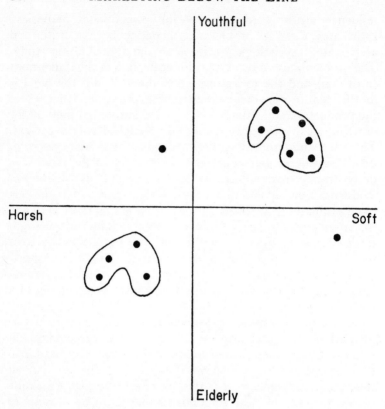

Figure 6.4. Product location in two-dimensional space

third, fourth, fifth, or any number of extra dimensions may be added. Obviously, searching for clusters in multi-dimensional space is not a feasible mechanical operation, but the computer has enabled such extremely complex taxonomic procedures to be performed on large data fields with many objects and many variables.

The advantage of using multi-dimensional analysis is that, unlike other methods, it does not rely on a series of dichotomies using a single segmentation criterion at a time, but rather it considers the market simultaneously in terms of all the stated dimensions.

In the same way that brands in the product field may be

grouped in terms of perceived similarity, so, too, may we group consumers or potential consumers. Indeed, such an analysis of brand positions will usually be run in tandem with a cluster analysis of consumer types. In this case, users of brands would be grouped according to their scores on a number of variables relating to their own psychological and personality characteristics. Such an analysis could result in the following clusters:[1]

(a) A habit determined group of brand-loyal customers.
(b) A cognitive group of consumers, sensitive to rational claims and only conditionally brand-loyal.
(c) A price-cognitive group, whose purchase decision is based mainly on price.
(d) An impulse group, basing their decision on the physical appeal of the brand.
(e) A group of emotional reactors, for whom symbols and images are the crux.
(f) A group of new consumers, not yet stabilized as regards the psychological dimensions of consumer behaviour.

Segmentation by attitudinal/psychological data alone, however, is open to the same criticisms voiced earlier, in that by looking at one aspect of consumer behaviour we are not encompassing the whole of the purchasing experience. Nevertheless, the methodology developed for multi-dimensional analysis, examined briefly in this section, may possibly provide a means for linking demographic usage and attitudinal/psychological information in a more realistic framework.

RESEARCH FINDINGS ON PROMOTIONAL SEGMENTS

U.S.A. Findings
Frank and Massy,[2] in a comprehensive study of household purchasing behaviour for a single food product in one major

---

[1] Woods, W., 'Psychological Dimensions of Consumer Decision', in *Journal of Marketing*, Vol. 24, No. 3 (1960).
[2] Massy, W. F., and Frank, R. E., 'Short Term Price and Dealing Effects in Selected Market Segments', in *Journal of Marketing Research*, Vol. II, pp. 171–185 (May 1965).

U.S.A. metropolitan area, over a 101-week period, examined the effects of demographic and socio-economic characteristics on customer response to promotions of a 'money-off' type. Their principal findings were:

(1) There is a reasonably significant relationship between the housewife's education and her response to such promotions. In general, these differences in response between the high and low education households seem to match the theory that the better educated respond more readily and adapt more quickly to change.

(2) There was a small relationship between the working status of the housewife and her promotional response, the working housewife being less responsive than the housewife at home. This accords with what one might reasonably have expected, the unemployed housewife possibly having a more flexible approach to shopping.

(3) Household income seemed to make little difference when it came to promotional response.

(4) The size of household and the age of the housewife appeared to have no effect on their participation in deals.

(5) There was some evidence that the 'heavy' buyers of the product tended to be more 'deal-prone'.

(6) Brand-loyalty seemed to have no effect on the housewife's response to promotions.

The findings of this study are disquieting, and in particular the reported phenomenon that customers who were loyal to the brand being studied tended to exhibit more or less the same response to 'money-off' deals as did those classified as non-loyal. The implication of this is that the promotions under study seemed to draw in existing brand-loyal users along with the others at whom, it is supposed, the promotion was aimed. It is difficult, however, to see how deals such as this can be confined to one target group when that target group is likely to cut across all socio-economic and demographic strata. Thus it is no use confining the promotion to specific regions, or to certain outlets, because it is assumed that brand-loyalty will occur among shoppers resident in all regions, and of different shopping habits.

Segmentation along demographic and usage criteria alone would appear in this instance to be unproductive.

The Deal-Prone Customer

It is sometimes suggested that certain consumers are more susceptible than others to below-the-line promotions, perhaps because of some motivational trait which is more likely to be activated by the offer of a promotion. The behavioural factors, discussed in Chapter Five, which are involved in the decision-making process are likely to achieve differential responses between people. However, the 'deal-prone' consumer has proved a most illusive object for the researcher to identify. It would appear that in different product/market situations, different types of people tend to be 'deal-prone'. Organizers of competitions do report that a small minority of the entries they attract are from habitual competition entrants (in fact, a *Competitor's Journal* exists in the United Kingdom).

Given that in particular situations a 'deal-prone' consumer does exist, how might he or she be identified? Webster[1] has suggested a method that is particularly useful in circumstances where continuous purchase data are available, as in the case of a Consumer Panel. This method enables the researcher to take into account the fact that some customers have more opportunity to take part in promotions than others; they may be heavy purchasers, for example, or the brand in question may have more promotions than others. In a typical market situation, where the consumer is likely to spread her purchases over a number of brands and over a long enough time period, the problem becomes even more involved.

Webster's Index of Deal-Proneness is derived as follows.

Let M = the number of consumers in the sample,
 $i = 1, \ldots m$
 N = the number of brands in the market,
 $j = 1, \ldots n$
 a_{ij} = the number of units of the jth brand purchased by the ith consumer.

[1] Webster, F. E., 'The "Deal-Prone" Consumer' *Journal of Marketing Research*, Vol. II, pp. 186–9 (May 1965).

Then:

$$\sum_{i=1}^{m} a_{ij} = s_j = \text{total sales of the } j\text{th brand to all consumers in the sample.}$$

$$\sum_{j=1}^{n} a_{ij} = P_i = \text{total purchases of the } i\text{th consumer.}$$

$$\sum_{j=1}^{n} s_j = \text{total sales of all brands of the product to all consumers in the sample.}$$

Now:

$$Q_j = \frac{s_j}{S} = \text{market share for the } j\text{th brand,}$$

where S = total sales of all brands to all sample consumers, and

$$R_j = \frac{a_{ij}}{P_i} = \text{consumer brand share to the } j\text{th brand,}$$

where

$$\sum_{j=1}^{n} R_j = 1 \quad 0 \leqslant R_j \leqslant 1$$

Now, let d_{ij} represent the number of units of the jth brand purchased by the ith consumer *on a deal basis*, and

$$d_{ij}/a_{ij} = C_{ij}$$

where

$$d_{ij} \leqslant a_{ij}$$

This measure, c_{ij}, gives the *percentage* of the ith consumer's purchases of the jth brand on a *deal basis*.

Finally, the number of units of the jth brand sold in the market, on a deal basis is given by:

$$\sum_{i=1}^{m} d_{ij} = D_j, \text{ total sales of the } j\text{th brand in units,}$$

and

$D_j/s_j = E_j$ percentage of deal sales to total sales for the jth brand,

where

$$D_j \leqslant s_j$$

The difference between c_{ij}, the percentage of the ith consumer's purchases of the jth brand made on a deal basis, and E_j, the percentage of the jth brand's sales made on a deal basis, is a measure of a propensity of the ith consumer to deal in the jth brand. Consumer brand share R_j is used as a weighting factor in order that the *opportunity* to deal in that brand may be taken into account. The resultant measure of a consumer's deal propensity for the jth brand is given by:

$$V_j = (C_{ij} - E_j)(R_j)$$

V_j can be either positive or negative—a consumer can purchase a brand either more or less frequently on a promotion than the frequency with which it is offered by the manufacturer.

The final measure of deal-proneness for the ith consumer is simply the summation of V_j's for that consumer. This measure, which Webster calls the Deal Proneness Index (D.P.I.), is given by:

$$\text{D.P.I.} = \sum_{j=1}^{n} V_j$$

and is a measure of the propensity of the consumer to buy the product class under consideration on a deal basis.

Webster's attempts to correlate deal-proneness with certain behavioural and purchasing characteristics were not particularly successful. He tentatively suggested that the deal-prone consumer is likely to be an older housewife who purchases fewer units but buys more brands and does not concentrate purchases on one brand.

Nevertheless, the D.P.I. provides an operational means for identifying the deal-prone consumer in a product/market situation. A feature of D.P.I. scores is that they should tend to be normally distributed, thus enabling the probability of a consumer having a particular D.P.I. score to be computed. With this feature in mind, it is possible to construct a distribution of sample scores from possible target groups for a promotion and compare them with the expected distribution, so providing a rough picture of the tendency towards deal-proneness in the particular group (Figure 6.5).

The Bradford/H.C.F. Study
A detailed picture of consumer preferences amongst the various

types of commonly used below-the-line promotions has been provided by the study of 1,000 United Kingdom housewives, carried out in the autumn of 1969, by the University of Bradford Management Centre, in association with Horniblow, Cox-Freeman Ltd. The intention of the study was to compare preferences and participation in promotions according to demographic, socio-economic, and attitudinal classifications in order to examine the potential for segmenting promotional effort along these lines.

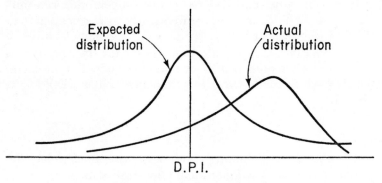

Figure 6.5. D.P.I. score distribution

The method of analysis was to compare responses amongst these classificatory groupings, according to respondents' stated preferences to a series of paired comparisons (see questionnaire, Appendix A). In this way it was possible to construct a hierarchy of preferences as stated by the respondents. Taking the preferences of all respondents together, the following ranking of promotions became apparent:

1. 'Money-off' type promotions
2. Extra quantity
3. Free sample
4. Coupons
5. Premium promotions
6. Free gift
7. { Competitions
    { Personality promotions

It can be seen (Figure 6.6) that 'money-off' type promotions

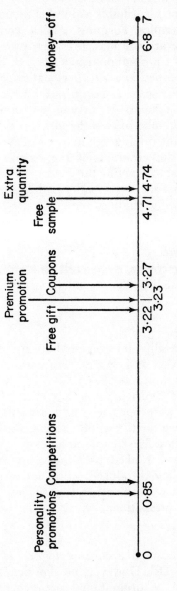

(Distance on the 0–7 continuum may be taken as corresponding to relative proximity of preference)

Figure 6.6. Relative preference for promotions

are by far the type most popular with the United Kingdom housewife. Following this are those types of promotion which most clearly represent identifiable value for money, i.e. extra quantity and free samples. Forming a fairly compact group lower down the scale are coupons, premium promotions, and free gifts. Of the eight promotional types tested, the two with lowest scores were competitions and personality promotions.

The validity of this scale is borne out by manufacturers' observations of the take-up of various promotional offers. Competitions, for example, have suffered a sizeable decline in recent years in the United Kingdom in terms of average entries.

Accepting, then, the accuracy of the paired comparison method, it is of interest to examine the differences in preferences between demographic, socio-economic, and attitudinal classifications. The following findings emerged from the cross-tabulation:

(1) *Age Group Differences*
In terms of stated preference, the overall ranking was the same for all age groups, matching the overall preference ranking discussed earlier.

(2) *Regional Differences*
Respondents were classified into regional groups; London and South-East, South-West and Wales, Midlands, North-West, North-East, and North, and Scotland.

It will be seen from Figure 6.7 that only minor differences in regional preferences were apparent, most regions conforming to the overall grouping for the whole sample. Midland housewives seemed to prefer a free sample to an extra quantity. The South-West and Wales ranked premium promotions higher than free gifts. Scotland produced scores for all promotions which were much closer to each other, thus suggesting a relative indifference between promotional types.

(3) *Social Class*
Respondents were classified according to one of two broad categories, ABC_1, C_2 DE. However, no significant differences were observed as far as promotional preferences were concerned.

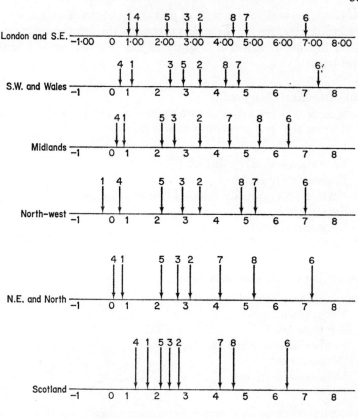

Key: 1. Personality promotion   5. Premium promotion
      2. Coupon   6. Money-off
      3. Free gift   7. Extra quantity
      4. Chance to enter a competition   8. Free sample

Figure 6.7. Pair groupings on a regional basis

(4) *Working Status*
Respondents were classified according to one of three categories; full-time work, part-time work, not working. No significant differences were observed.

(5) *Family Type*
Respondents were classified according to one of two categories; with children, without children. Taking the mean scores for

all classifications, for each set of pair comparisons, no significant variation emerges for these two groups, although the deviation from the mean scores is slightly higher for that group with children.

(6) *Attitudinal Classification*

Respondents were asked to rate themselves along two five-point scales; on the first according to whether they were:

Very economically minded
Economically minded
Neither economically minded nor extravagant
Extravagant
Very extravagant

in terms of their shopping behaviour. On the second scale, according to whether they were:

Very adventurous
Adventurous
Neither adventurous nor conservative
Conservative
Very conservative

in terms of their innovative behaviour. Again no significant variation emerged from this cross-tabulation.

The conclusions to be drawn from the Bradford/H.C.F. Study of consumer preferences seemed to offer little hope for segmentation along traditional lines. When below-the-line promotions are ranked on preference, irrespective of more detailed classifications such as age and region, *money-off offers* are always the type of promotion most preferred. Of the remaining types of promotions included in the study, preferences generally fall into three main groups. The differences between each of the four clusterings of promotion on the overall scales are significant and remain so for most of the cross-tabulations. Regional differences, where they appear, are significant, but working status, family type, age, and the attitudinal classification used, appear only to influence marginally these variations.

PARTICIPATION

The Bradford/H.C.F. Study also attempted to gather data on *participation* in below-the-line promotions by consumers. The most striking feature to arise out of the data was the almost universally low participation in promotions of all types. In response to the question: 'Could you estimate how many promotions of one sort or another you participated in during the last six months?' the median number of promotions quoted by the total 1,011 housewives was approximately five, i.e. less than one per month.

It does seem, however, that most housewives were interpreting the question to mean *active* participation in a promotion, i.e. they were not including money-off offers and the like, but rather were referring to promotions where either they were required to send off to the manufacturers or their agents, or that there was a promotion, such as a banded pack, that was easily remembered. Because of the distortion due to a likely inability to cast one's mind back over the whole of the six months, this figure is probably misleading, and most likely understates the true total. Nevertheless, whilst the total figure may be distorted, it is likely that these distortions were common to all respondents and we are therefore justified in making comparisons between the various demographic and socio-economic groups within the total. It is in these inter-group comparisons that some interesting features emerge.

VARIATIONS IN PARTICIPATION

As seen in Figure 6.8, 70 per cent of the total respondents claimed to have taken part in less than fifteen promotions, of one sort or another, over the last six months, and only 17 per cent stated more than 25. With this figure in mind it is useful to compare deviations from this figure in the various sub-groupings.

Age
In the group 16–24 years, 22 per cent of the respondents claimed to have taken part in more than 25 promotions, and in the 25–34 age group this figure rose to 34 per cent. In other words, the

under-35's seem to be the predominant group in their participation in promotions.

Social Class
There would appear to be no significant difference between the two groupings.

Working Status
Small differences appear here, but these are likely to be due to sampling errors.

Family
Twenty-two per cent of housewives with children claimed to have participated in more than 25 promotions over the period, whereas only 14 per cent of those without children had participated in the same number.

Region
It is in the regional breakdown that the most dramatic differences seem to occur. To take the extreme example, only 1 per cent of Scottish housewives had taken part in over 25 promotions, whilst 45 per cent of housewives in the North-West of England claimed to have done so. Similarly, whilst 34 per cent of Scottish housewives had taken part in no promotions at all, no North-West housewife fell into this category. This striking difference is shown on the cumulative percentage diagram (Figure 6.8).

A similar, although not quite as dramatic, difference shows up in the figures of those claiming to have taken part in 25 or more in London and the South-East (10 per cent), and in the North and North-East (23 per cent).

It would appear therefore, that there is a regional pattern to promotion-participation. The South and Midlands are below average, whilst the North of England generally is well above. Scotland, with a median number of promotions participated in of less than 1, is clearly far below the nationwide average.

OTHER GROUPINGS

Attempts were made to group the housewives according to

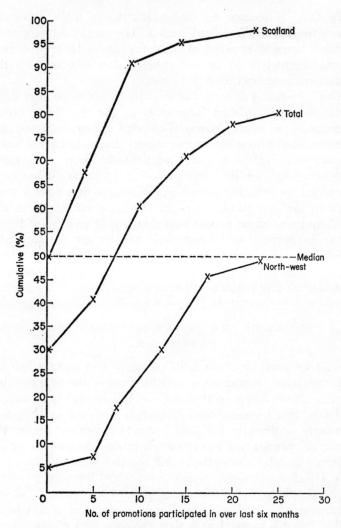

Figure 6.8. Cumulative participation in promotions in selected areas

where they placed themselves on the following dimensions of purchasing behaviour:

Economy-minded—Extravagant
Adventurous—Conservative

In fact, it seemed to make remarkably little difference where the housewife placed herself. The results for economy-minded housewives were broadly similar to those who perceived themselves to be extravagant and similarly on the adventurous–conservative dimension.

One interesting feature did emerge, however, in that those housewives who placed themselves in the middle of either dimension, i.e. neither economy-minded nor extravagant, and neither adventurous nor conservative, tended to have a lower participation in promotions, particularly those who rated themselves neither adventurous nor conservative. It has been suggested that placing oneself in the middle of a bipolar scale such as this is a passive act, not requiring committal in any way, and that those people who don't want to commit themselves by actively describing their actions are the sort who would not want actively to commit themselves by taking part in a promotion. Whilst being an interesting hypothesis, it would obviously require further testing.

A PROFILE OF THE UNITED KINGDOM PROMOTION PARTICIPANT

Whilst we must be cautious in attempting to make a blanket generalization, it does seem, on the basis of the participation figures above, that several major conclusions may be drawn.

In the first instance, the low overall levels for participation probably understate the true picture: in other words, the housewife cannot recollect the small in-store promotion, or the 'penny-off' offer. Nevertheless, if recalled participation is so low, could it not follow that the perceived importance of the promotion in her decision-making process is low also? This is a controversial hypothesis, and is merely stated here as a possibility. What is more clear is that the *active* type of promotion, i.e. promotion involving a definite commitment by the housewife such as saving tokens or sending money for a gift, is not being entered into in quite the numbers that manufacturers would like to think.

If there is a group of housewives who are heavy participants in promotions, then they probably have the following profile: they are under 35 years old, they have one child or more at home, and they live in the North, the North-West, or the North-East of England.

Table 6.1. *Regional variations in participation*

		Region					
No. of promotions	Total (%)	London and S.E. (%)	South-West and Wales (%)	Mid-lands (%)	North-West (%)	North-East and North (%)	Scot-land (%)
None	17	17	18	23	—	15	34
1–5	24	29	19	26	6	21	32
6–10	20	22	22	17	13	19	25
11–15	9	9	12	8	10	8	5
16–20	7	6	7	9	15	5	3
21–25	3	4	2	1	5	7	—
More than 25	17	10	19	13	45	23	1
D.K.	3	3	1	3	6	2	—
Base	1013	351	130	163	126	150	92

CONCLUSIONS

A number of possibilities seem to present themselves to the promotional planner considering a strategy of market segmentation. In the first instance, a number of useful analogies and techniques from advertising management may have applications below-the-line. The principle of defining target audiences for media advertising can be carried through to promotional planning; what segments of the market are we trying to reach, and what would be the response to a specific promotion of members of this target audience? This question, carefully answered, could result in a higher degree of promotional cost-effectiveness. The problem is, of course, that to provide the answer to this question for a specific product/market situation requires considerable research—what is the proportion of deal-prone customers in the total market, do they form recognizable segments, can they be approached with a minimum of overlap with other segments?

This chapter has presented a number of leads for a differentiated approach to promotional planning. What is now required is hard research to put some factual flesh on what are

TABLE 6.2. *Number of promotions participated in during last 6 months*

No. of promotions	Total (%)	Age groups				Social class		Working status			Family	
		16–24 (%)	25–34 (%)	35–44 (%)	45+ (%)	ABC_1 (%)	C_1DE (%)	Full-time (%)	Part-time (%)	Non-work (%)	With child (%)	No child (%)
None	17	20	14	11	19	15	18	18	15	17	14	19
1–5	24	19	21	29	24	28	21	24	20	24	24	24
6–10	20	17	21	20	20	20	20	21	20	19	18	21
11–15	9	9	8	7	10	9	9	8	12	8	8	10
16–20	7	7	10	10	6	5	8	7	8	7	9	6
21–25	3	3	2	3	4	2	4	3	3	3	3	3
More than 25	17	22	24	18	14	19	17	16	20	19	22	14
D.K.	3	3	—	2	3	2	3	3	2	3	2	3
Base	1012	90	169	178	573	349	662	211	172	629	394	616

largely theoretical bones. It seems surprising, in an age when expenditure on below-the-line promotion equals or exceeds expenditure on above-the-line, that very little is spent on research below-the-line compared with that on above.

Experience of the promotional process below-the-line quite clearly demonstrates that segmentation of the market for a product, on a multi-dimensional basis, and in terms of differential response to below-the-line, is possible and can be highly profitable.

CHAPTER SEVEN

PROMOTIONS AND THE IMAGE

THE power of the 'image' has long been an area of attention among academics and marketing practitioners alike. The psychology of perception, a subject in itself, is a complex and controversial area. One thing, though, is accepted, that objects quite often carry connotations that are not reflections of physical or innate attributes alone. In other words, our perception and ultimately our evaluation of the object is coloured by the associations that the object produces in our mind. We call these associations the 'image'. Certain symbols, too, will have the same connotative power: a swastika or the hammer and sickle, for example, will arouse particular emotions.

In a less dramatic, yet nevertheless pervasive way, the company and its brands will have an image in the eyes of its publics. This image may be strong or it may be weak, it may work in favour of the company or it may work against it and different sections of the company's publics may interpret the image in different ways.

It is usual to distinguish between *corporate* and *brand* image. Corporate image may be defined as the spontaneous idea of the company generally based on slender precepts gained from a subjective contact with the company, its products, reputation, and promotional mix. On the other hand, the brand image relates to a specific product in the company's product line:

> The Brand Image may be defined as the set of associations which a brand has acquired for a given person—as a result of exposure to the advertising, hearsay, and perhaps actual experience of the brand—with particular functions, qualities, characteristics of its users and their homes, and so on.[1]

[1] John Downing, 'What is a Brand Image?' *The Advertising Quarterly*, No. 2 (1964).

Images, therefore, both at the corporate and at the brand level are an amorphous constellation of feelings, which may differ widely from person to person. What is important about this is that the image can be a major determinant in consumer acceptance and purchase of a company's product. A company with a strong and acceptable corporate image may still have a brand with an unacceptable image to a major segment of the market. A prime purpose of marketing activity is to build the image of the brand, and indeed, one hopes, the corporate image, to give it values in the eyes of the consumer and to guard this image over time.

The promotional strategist must therefore take cognizance of the wider image considerations, as his actions conceivably could damage brand and/or corporate image and thus erode the basis of the company's acceptance in its markets.

THE EFFECT OF PROMOTIONS ON THE IMAGE

Clearly, corporate image and brand image are powerful and important determinants in the purchase process. The more that this image can be strengthened and moved towards the consumers' ideal image, the greater is the likelihood of purchase. It is the purpose of corporate communications to attempt a drawing together of actual and ideal. A corporate communications programme should perfectly be a total, company-wide approach which embraces theme advertising, corporate advertising, below-the-line promotion, corporate design, and public relations. The advantages of such an integrated approach have been examined in Chapter Five, and clearly it makes sense for all the activities affecting corporate and brand images to be closely co-ordinated.

There can be little doubt that below-the-line promotion can affect the company image. The effect can be either favourable or unfavourable. Shell in the United Kingdom have for many years run what amounts to a series of promotions in the form of books on the British countryside, calendars illustrating the country at different times of the year, and so on. These promotions are corporate promotions, they are not aimed at increasing sales of petrol and oil directly, but rather work as a part of a continuing public relations effort. On the other hand, a promotion can be harmful to the corporate image. Goods offered in a premium promotion which, when received, turn out to be shoddy or do not seem to be as grand as the promotional copy might have suggested could have a considerable negative influence on the consumer's attitude towards that company and all its products. The important feature here is that an adverse opinion of one product can be transferred to other brands in the company's product line—more so if the corporate symbol, trademark, or name is stressed on individual brands.

The effect on the brand image of promotions can be even greater than the effect on the corporate image. We will examine later in this chapter the possible long-term effects of promotions on the 'saleability' of the brand, but there are some initial factors concerning the impact on image that need to be considered. The brand that uses promotions creatively, tying in with the 'personality' of the brand, is more likely to enhance its image in the eyes of the customer. A promotion can give an existing image a boost. For example, the hardworking, efficient image of a detergent could be given a little warmth and humanity by the offer of washable framed prints of flowers, suitable for the kitchen. On the other hand, too many of the wrong sort of promotions can dull the image of the brand; a series of money-off offers is almost a guarantee that the image of the brand will come to be tinged with 'cheapness', and all that this means to the consumer.

Research in the United States has demonstrated the effect in a specific instance of a promotion on brand image.[1] In this case the experiment illustrated the effect of a free sample in changing the image of a product from one that was previously 'feminine' to one of 'masculinity'. The researchers reported:

> There is a definite indication that if a product has a feminine image in the eyes of men, exposure to a free sample is very likely to change the image. Furthermore, such an exposure is likely to create a more favourable attitude towards the product and increase the intention to buy.

Implications of the findings for marketing management are numerous:

[1] Hamm, B. C., Perry, M., and Wynn, H. F., 'The Effect of a Free Sample on Image and Attitude', in *Journal of Advertising Research*, Vol. 9, No. 4, 1969.

(1) It has been found that products have a sex image and there are consumers who see products as feminine or masculine. This image is important because it indicates the limitations of the market and one way of segmenting it.

(2) The sex image is subject to changes; it is a dynamic concept that can be altered or modified.

(3) One efficient way of changing the image of a product is by distributing a free sample and presenting the product as being different from predisposed images. This method was found to be successful, although there was no proof of actual product use.

(4) Free sample distribution is helpful in improving attitudes towards the product and increasing the intention to buy.

THE CONCEPT OF SALEABILITY

Recently there has developed a school of thought which has suggested that the role of promotion, and advertising in particular, is not so much to influence sales directly but to make the product more saleable by adding value to it. In other words, the power of promotion lies in its ability to affect the *gestalt* of a product, to give it intangible qualities that it did not have before. It is, in fact, the process that changes a product into a brand.

Grahame Leman[1] has expressed this view succinctly:

It is widely urged that short run sales results are the only acceptable ... index of the effectiveness of advertising. I [would] argue that long run profit results may in many ways be a better index—or, which amounts to the same thing— that advertising adds value, affects saleability, rather than sales.

Saleability, then, is that quality that makes the brand desirable to the consumer. The higher is the brand's saleability, the higher the likelihood of its purchase. Advertising, it is argued, can, through the message it carries, add to the saleability of the product by giving it added values. Promotions, on the other hand, may detract from this saleability by devaluing

[1] Leman, Grahame, *Sales, Saleability and the Saleability Gap*, B.B.T.A. Monograph (1969).

the brand's values in the eyes of the customer. It is this latter possibility that we must examine. At the same time, the expenditure of funds below-the-line necessarily means that there is less available for the substantial accretion of saleability via theme advertising.

Can promotions devalue the brand? It certainly seems plausible that, for example, a successive number of price-cut type offers, which appear to the customer to amount virtually to a continuous reduction, could possibly lead the consumer to view this as a cheap, or cheaper product. Whether this 'cheapening' of the brand, as perceived by the consumer, would have an effect on purchasing behaviour would depend on the nature of the product and the market. The use of price by the potential consumer as an indicator of quality is a well-known phenomenon.[1] If a brand is perceived to continuously carry money-off offers, this may lead, for example, to a feeling by the consumer about the brand that 'they are having to reduce the price in order to sell it', i.e. as in a sale.

The wrong sort of promotion can damage the brand. There is obviously a need to match the promotion to the nature of the brand and its consumers. One would not offer plastic daffodils with expensive Chateau-bottled wine, whereas they might be appropriate for a soap powder. If saleability is created through the added values imparted by theme advertising, then it is possible that it could be reduced through inappropriate promotions and by not sustaining theme support. This effect will inevitably be long-term in the sense that only over time would the effects of inappropriate promotions be manifested in declining brand share, unfavourable changes in attitudes towards the brand, and so on:

Otherwise put, straight advertising and allied activities may gradually change the world into one in which the product is more saleable (or, at least, prevent the world from changing into one in which the product is less saleable); promotion, exploiting the world as it finds it, for quick returns, may only leave the world unchanged (or even change it into a world in which the product is less saleable than it was). Moreover,

[1] Gabor, André, and Granger, C. W. J., 'Price as an Indicator of Quality: Report on an Inquiry', *Economica*, Vol. 33 (February 1966).

since money spent on exploitation cannot also be spent on creation, the two effects are not accidentally coincident, but necessarily intertwined.

(Leman, *op. cit.*)

Mention has been made of the parallel danger that exists to saleability through below-the-line promotion activity reducing the total budget available for theme advertising. Stephen King[1] has illustrated such an affect on one brand. Delsey and Andrex are two major brands of soft toilet paper retailing in the United Kingdom. They were responsible between themselves for opening up the United Kingdom soft toilet paper market. In the early 1960s the success of these two brands led to a growth in the number of smaller, cheaper brands being offered —many of them as private labels. Delsey decided to counter this by switching its total promotional activity away from theme advertising towards trade discounting. In fact, by 1967 Delsey's advertising was negligible (Figure 7.1), but it was very actively discounting to the trade. Meanwhile, Andrex had maintained a balance between the two activities.

The result of this strategy has been that Delsey have slipped back considerably in its market share whilst private labels and smaller manufacturers have continued to grow, but, more interestingly, Andrex has also improved its market share (Figure 7.2).

Research has shown that attitudes towards Delsey, when compared with those towards Andrex, have moved unfavourably, although there has been no noticeable change in the quality of either brand (Figure 7.3).

The conclusion that may be drawn from this is that there is a clear reduction in the *saleability* of Delsey. With little or no theme support to add value to the brand, it was clearly at a disadvantage to Andrex, which was able to create a specific 'personality' for the product which transcended its mere functional qualities.

Whether the decline of Delsey was due to (a) its use of below-the-line, (b) the reduction of its theme advertising, or (c) a combination of both, depends on one's point of view. Whatever the case, it is self-evident that below-the-line promotion, either

[1] King, Stephen, Address to the Advertising Association Conference, 1970.

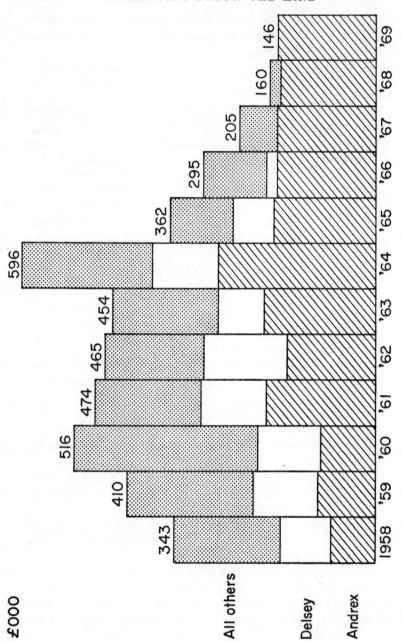

£000

Figure 7.1. Toilet paper: advertising expenditure. (*Source*: Legion, Meal)

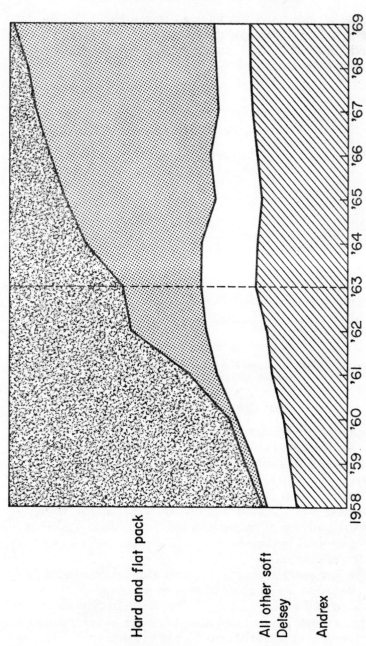

Hard and flat pack

All other soft
Delsey

Andrex

1958 '59 '60 '61 '62 '63 '64 '65 '66 '67 '68 '69

[Figure 7.2. Toilet paper: market shares (volume basis). (*Source*: Nielsen)

directly or indirectly, can have an undesirable effect on the long-term brand share. Whether this is due to a sapping of the brand's saleability or for some other reason has yet to be conclusively demonstrated.

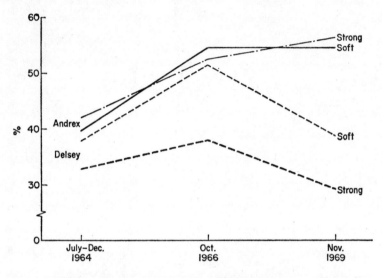

Figure 7.3. Changes in attitude to Andrex and Delsey (percentage of housewives attributing to each brand) (*Source*: API)

CHOOSING THE RIGHT PROMOTION

A number of considerations are involved when it comes to choosing the actual form the promotion should take, once it has been decided that some form of below-the-line activity would be appropriate. In Chapter Three, suggestions were made as to how various types of promotion could be used to meet specific marketing objectives. In addition to the relatively straightforward matching of promotions and objectives, it is necessary to get involved in considerations of the promotion's impact on the brand's saleability.

The first essential here is to ensure that the 'dimensions' of the promotion are in accordance with the 'dimensions' of the product and the market. By dimensions we mean those attributes of the product, physical and abstract, which are perceived by the consumer or potential consumer to be relevant in his or her purchase decision. Is the product, for example, perceived to be a 'luxury' that is purchased as an indulgence, does it have connotations of high life and good living? Or is it an everyday sort of purchase, but one which is mainly purchased by careful, caring and sensible mothers? Whatever the dimensions may be, it is critical that the promotion is in key with them; 2½p. off may not go down too well with the first example of a luxury product, whilst a competition offering at sensual fortnight's holiday in Bali might—and vice versa—for the latter product. Whilst these observations are commonsense, there are a remarkable number of promotions being offered at any point in time which simply do not match the product/ market situation. Equally important is the need to ensure that the promotion is of a type likely to appeal to the target audience in terms of participation. There must be a propensity on the part of these consumers to participate in that type of promotion. The actual identification of what are relevant dimensions to the consumer will usually require field research if an objective basis for promotional planning is to be achieved.

Every successful brand has a 'personality'. The personality of a brand is a function of its advertising, its package, perhaps its physical attributes, and so on. Generally, too, this brand personality will be consistent as far as its perception by the consumer is concerned, although a personality which may appeal to one person may not appeal to another. It is a similar sort of process to the way we make friends; either we like the aggressive personality of Brand X or we find it distasteful. Some useful information about how consumers and potential consumers perceive a brand's personality can be obtained from simple research, by asking them to imagine if certain brands, including the one under study, were people, what sorts of personalities would they have.

The theme strategy, too, should be paramount in determining the form promotion should take. Given that the role of theme advertising is to give added value to the brand, it follows that sales promotions should be tailored in with the theme in order that they, too, may 'add value'. There is no inherent reason why promotions should detract from long-run saleability (other than through a leaching of funds from the above-the-line appropriation) and, used judiciously, they could even add to it.

H

CHAPTER EIGHT

ASSESSING PROMOTIONAL COST EFFECTIVENESS

THE manager concerned with the allocation of resources must also be concerned with the evaluation of the effectiveness of this allocation. However, as 'effectiveness', yet to be defined, may be gained by the expenditure of large sums of money it is necessary to set the response achieved against the cost involved. Thus we may view the resource allocation problem as one of maximizing the output (perhaps measured in terms of sales) from a given input, usually measured in terms of cost. For many purposes, a crude ratio of sales to cost of sales may be sufficient to assess the various allocation possibilities open to the manager. This approach, however, ignores the success or otherwise of the programme in meeting its initial stated objectives. Thus, for promotional expenditures we must be concerned not only with the cost of sales achieved but with the cost of achieving promotional objectives which are likely to involve considerations other than sales.

In many cases, because of the problems outlined in preceding chapters, it is difficult to separate the effects of below-the-line promotion from all the other elements in the total communications mix. Indeed, to attempt to make individual analyses of promotional effectiveness may lead the manager into ignoring the interactions and synergy potential of an integrated promotional programme.

We may discern ten basic steps for a cost-effectiveness study which, carried out in this way, can provide a useful decision tool for deciding on a promotional programme before a commitment to allocate resources is embarked upon:[1]

---

[1] This procedure is adapted from that given by A. D. Kazanowski in Chapter Seven of *Cost Effectiveness*, J. M. English (ed.), (Wiley, New York, 1968).

(1) Define the desired goals, objectives, missions, or purposes that the promotional programme is to meet or fulfil.

(2) Identify the promotional requirements essential to the attainment of the desired goals.

(3) Develop alternative promotional programmes for accomplishing the objectives.

(4) Establish programme evaluation criteria (measures) that relate promotional capabilities to the programme requirements.

(5) Select a fixed-cost or fixed-effectiveness approach. In other words, do we wish to achieve the best possible results from a given fixed expenditure, or do we wish to achieve a certain level of effectiveness at a minimum cost?

(6) Determine capabilities of the alternative programmes in terms of the evaluation criteria.

(7) Generate a programme-versus-criteria array, i.e. a matrix of possible outcomes and their effectiveness.

(8) Analyse the merits of alternative programmes.

(9) Perform sensitivity analysis, i.e. determine the change in outcome generated by a given change in inputs.

(10) Document the rationale, assumptions, and analyses underlying the previous nine stages.

This last step is particularly important in that it forces the manager to question the basis of his judgement and may possibly produce changes in his original criteria of promotional effectiveness or other basic precepts.

Certain measurement devices are available to the manager enabling this assessment procedure to be carried through. Basic to these methods is the concept of sales response to promotional input.

PROMOTIONAL RESPONSE FUNCTIONS

Diminishing returns to additional inputs after a certain level of input is a phenomenon encountered in almost every productive system, be it the production of toothpaste or of a motor car. In the same way there is a definite relationship between promotional inputs and the response in the form of sales. Common-sense would tell us that the response of sales to advertising is unlikely to be linear, that is, £300,000 worth of advertising would not produce three times as many sales as £100,000. It may, in fact, produce less than three times as much, or more. The scale of the return—diminishing, increasing, or proportional—depends upon the cumulative effect on the consumer and potential consumer of what has gone before. Advertising research has demonstrated that the general form of this response function, if graphed, is an S-shape. That is, until a certain threshold is passed, advertising does not seem to have any effect; for example, spending only £1,000 a year on advertising in a highly competitive mass market is unlikely to make any impact on sales. Once the threshold is passed, the cumulative effect of promotion begins to show through. The effects of advertising are not always immediate, and the slow build-up leads to a lagged effect in many marketing situations. This can be confusing to the analyst attempting to assess promotional cost-effectiveness. After a while, however, no matter how much extra is injected into the promotional appropriation sales increase less than proportionately and diminishing returns are in evidence. This could occur because the existing market has reached its saturation level, or because the repetition of an advertising message may eventually numb rather than excite. Typically, therefore, we may postulate a curve with the characteristics of Figure 8.1.

Similarly, it can be demonstrated that the same non-proportional effects exist in below-the-line promotion as well as with theme advertising. It would be misleading, however, to think in terms of a single aggregate response function for all below-the-line expenditures. Instead, it is necessary to construct response functions for specific promotions to specific recipients, for example, a deal to a retailer or a premium offer to the housewife. Because of the more immediate impact of below-the-line, however, it is possible that the 'toe' of the S-curve in fact is non-existent, or at least only vestigial, and there is no threshold effect. But following on from this may be a situation where diminishing returns set in sooner—there is perhaps a limit to the promotional activity that the recipient is prepared to participate in. A promotions/sales response function may typically therefore, take on a form such as that in Figure 8.2. Response functions such as these represent only the relatively

short-term promotional effects and assume no lengthy dis-
continuities or major fluctuations in promotional expenditure.

The importance of attempting to plot response functions will
be apparent. If the marketing analyst wishes to assess the
marginal effectiveness of an extra promotional pound, then it

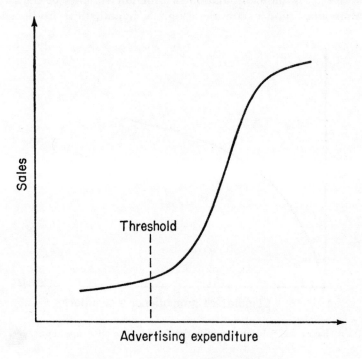

Figure 8.1. Advertising/sales response function

becomes necessary to know just where on the curve the brand
is, and what slope the curve is taking from there on. Whilst the
description of these curves has been oversimplified, it is possible
operationally to derive them with a reasonable degree of
accuracy using regression and other curve-fitting techniques.

Having some idea of the relative form of the response functions
for promotional types makes the manager's task of inter-type
comparison easier. It is rare that one promotional type is used
to the exclusion of all others. Somewhere there is an optimal
cost-effective combination of different promotions which will

produce the highest sales/cost ratio. Conceptually, this may be presented as a problem of combining two promotional inputs and then generalizing to the number actually available.

The first step in such an analysis is the derivation of iso-benefit curves, showing how the same sales effect may be achieved by the combination of different volumes of the two promotions under consideration. A hypothetical iso-benefit

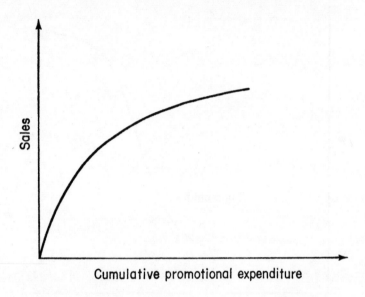

Figure 8.2. Sales response function for premium offer expenditure

curve may look like that displayed in Figure 8.3. There are obviously an infinitesimal number of such curves in any one situation; they may be exactly parallel to one another, or they may change shape as different combinations of promotional expenditures are considered (Figure 8.4).

The promotional allocation problem is to find for a given iso-benefit curve that point which involves the minimum total cost. Thus in Figure 8.5 combination X produces a total cost equal to the sum $a_1 + b_1$, whilst combination Y produces a total cost equal to $a_2 + b_2$. It is not too difficult to find the approximate location by graphic means of this least-cost combination. The problem in implementing this procedure lies in the collection of sufficient experimental data to produce a valid iso-benefit curve for a given product/market situation.

Experimentation, in fact, is the key to many of the questions surrounding the assessment of promotional effectiveness, and later in this chapter specific experimental procedures will be described.

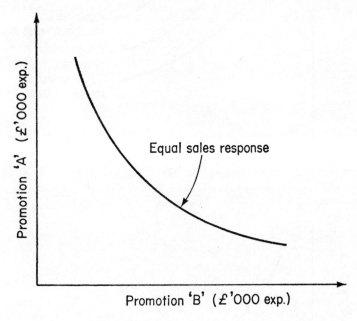

Figure 8.3. Iso-benefit curve

In the end, the Marketing Manager will probably have to accept less than perfect information about comparative cost-effectiveness of promotions, and will have to look instead at the response of sales to the total company promotional expenditure.

THE TOTAL PROMOTIONAL COST/BENEFIT AUDIT

Too often, promotional effectiveness is measured only in terms of extra sales, be it a short-term volume improvement or a longer-term increase in brand share. The effect of promotions, however, may be more widely felt throughout the company's

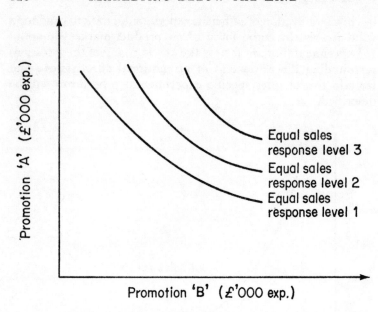

Figure 8.4

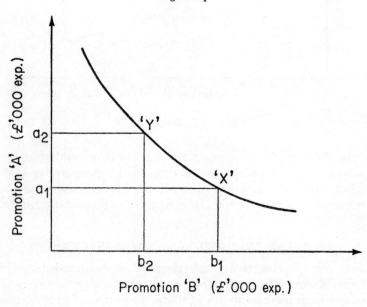

Figure 8.5

operations, in particular upon production scheduling and inventory allocation. The effectiveness of promotions must therefore be measured in cost/benefit terms, i.e. an assessment needs to be made of the impact, in cost terms, upon every aspect of the business.

An example of how a sales promotion can affect production and inventory is given below. This demonstrates the need for a careful co-ordination between the operations side of the business —for example, purchasing, production, and distribution—and the marketing and sales side. All too often it is the case that co-ordination between marketing and production is minimal, if it exists at all.

AN EXAMPLE OF PROMOTIONAL/OPERATIONS INTERACTION

The XYZ company sells, amongst other things, a range of tea. From time to time, one of these is promoted by one of a variety of methods. In this particular example, there had been no major promotion for six months, and sales, measured in terms of consumer offtake, were fairly constant. After a careful examination of the situation, the Marketing Manager decided that a suitable money-off promotion should be launched to attempt to bring in new purchasers. The promotion was launched, and in the immediate post-launch period consumer sales went up by 10 per cent. However, as it transpired, most of these extra sales were in fact provided by existing customers 'stocking up' with the product in order to take advantage of the offer. In the following time period, therefore, sales dropped considerably below the norm, reaching a low point of 7 per cent below the norm, whilst these stocks were being consumed. Eventually, sales caught up again to consolidate at a level 3 per cent above the original norm. The consumer sales history took the form shown in Figure 8.6.

Because of stock-holding in the distribution channel, any change in final consumer demand is magnified somewhat by the time it reaches the production line. In the case of XYZ company, a distribution channel of wholesaler to retailer to consumer was used. At each level in the channel, various stock-holding policies were in operation. For example, the retailers generally held about 3 weeks' supply as stock, the wholesalers held 8 weeks' supply, and the manufacturer's warehouse about 6 weeks' stock.

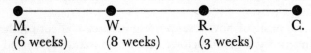

M. = Manufacturer.
W. = Wholesaler.
R. = Retailer.
C. = Consumer.

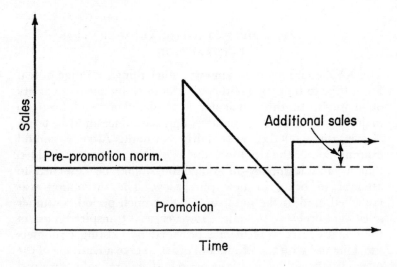

Figure 8.6. Consumer offtake

Now if the retailer experiences an increase in consumer demand of 10 per cent and if he wishes to maintain his stock level, then the order he places with the wholesaler will be greater than 10 per cent (it needs to be 10 per cent + 10 per cent (3/52) i.e. 10·6 per cent). This increased demand is passed on by the wholesaler after being further magnified (10·6 per cent + 10·6 per cent (8/52) i.e. 12·2 per cent) and finally the manufacturer's warehouse requests a new level of production of 13·6 per cent over the norm (12·2 per cent + 12·2 per cent (6/52)).

In the following time period, of course, sales dropped 7 per cent below the norm representing a fall in consumer demand in this period over the last of 17 per cent. The decrease in demand, according to the same assumptions, is multiplied through the marketing channel to produce a fall in production requirements of approximately 23 per cent. The final upward adjustment to the new norm produces an increase in production requirements of 13·6 per cent. Figure 8.7 illustrates these fluctuations.

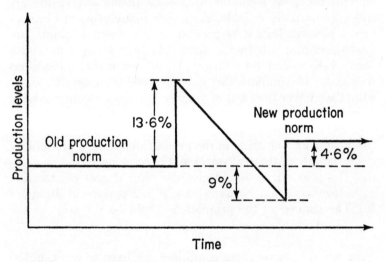

Figure 8.7. Fluctuations in production demand

This little-known effect, whilst never being as easy to plot as in this hypothetical example, is clearly of some importance. Fluctuations of any type in a production schedule are costly, and these costs should be taken into account when evaluating the total effect of a promotion. Careful co-ordination between marketing and production can, in fact, reduce these fluctuations and lead to a better utilization of production resources.

PRE-TESTING PROMOTIONS

Ideally, one would wish to subject all proposed promotions to a series of tests *before* they were actually used in a marketing programme in order to determine:

(1) What is the most suitable promotion to achieve the promotional objectives?
(2) What will be the short-term effect on sales?
(3) What will be the long-term effects on the brand's personality and 'saleability'?

Unfortunately present-day research technology is not equal to the task of providing the complete answers to these questions. Indeed, the tools available to pre-test theme advertising are still only partially reliable, even after many years of development. Nevertheless, it is possible to lay down a number of guide-lines that will enable the Marketing Manager to reduce some of the uncertainty. Generally, the purpose of the pre-test should be to simulate the market-place situation. In other words, whatever the form of test, the following conditions must be met:

(a) People participating in the pre-test should be a probability sample of the real world audience.
(b) The respondent should give the same degree of attention to the promotion as she would in a real world situation.
(c) The context of the promotion should be the same as the real world context.

In practice, these three conditions are hard to meet, unless the test takes the form of a controlled experiment where the promoted product is put on limited sale. This approach will be discussed in more detail later in the chapter.

Nevertheless, if a crude and possibly inaccurate estimate of a promotion's ability to meet its objectives and an assessment of its sales effects is acceptable, it is possible to relax the foregoing conditions somewhat.

Essentially, in the first instance the researcher should be seeking qualitative information. He will need to know about the basic 'constructs' of consumer reactions to promotions, i.e. what are the relevant dimensions when it comes to consumer evaluation of promotions? The long-term considerations will involve an examination of the perceived 'personality' of the brand, and how this is likely to be affected by the proposed promotion. Again this information is purely qualitative, and is likely to be derived via group discussions of a non-structured type.

One technique which has possibilities here is the 'shopping bag' approach. Here two matched groups of housewives are shown the contents of a shopping bag. The contents would be identical for both groups, except that one of the products in the second bag would have a promotion of some sort clearly visible. The housewives would then be asked to describe the nature of the shopper who had purchased the products in the shopping bag. This projective technique has worked well on similar experiments and usually produces two sets of descriptions which, by their differences, can give insights into consumers' reactions to specific brands, or, in this case, promotions.

Differences in reaction to promotions of different types can perhaps be adduced more simply by asking respondents, suitably selected to represent the target group, to state their preferences. Using a method of paired comparisons, a rating scale for these promotions may be built up.

In all these tests, however, it is essential that the promotion is not separated from the brand. It is the *total* effect of one upon the other that the researcher should be interested in. Assessing these interactions, which are largely intangible, is the chief problem in non-experimental pre-tests of promotion.

EXPERIMENTAL PROMOTIONAL PRE-TESTS

The experimental approach to marketing research is a source of great potential in the determination of cause and effect. Theoretically, an experimental approach could attempt to examine all combinations of all relevant variables in order that the various interactions involved when variables are working together could be uncovered. However, the fact that the number of variables and thus the number of combinations is frequently very large precludes this grand-scale investigation. If the researcher is prepared to forgo the knowledge of some of these interactions it is possible to produce *experimental designs* that can still give insight into cause and effect.

In the experimental approach to marketing we are introducing stimuli over which we have control regarding their magnitude, duration, etc., into a particular situation and then comparing the effect that these stimuli have on behaviour. In order that we may reduce the possibility of misinterpreting the results, it is necessary to observe concurrently behaviour in an exactly similar situation with no experimental inputs. Thus, in an experiment to compare the relative effectiveness in short-term sales of two promotions the experimenter, in a single experiment, might select three exactly similar shops in exactly similar locations, with exactly similar clientele, and in one shop

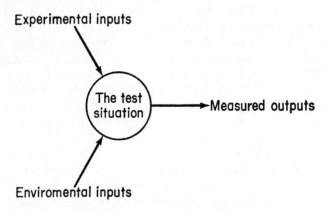

Figure 8.8. The experimental situation

place Promotion A, in the second shop Promotion B, and in the third shop the brand would be sold unpromoted. The difference in sales could then be noted, and, all other things being equal, the effect on each promotion ascertained. The purpose of this third shop, or 'control' is to take cognizance of what may be termed *environmental* effects, for example, competitive action. Figure 8.8 shows the experiment visualized as a system.

An example of the use to which this type of experiment can be put in evaluating the effects of below-the-line promotion on sales is illustrated by an experiment carried out by the U.S. Department of Agriculture.[1] The purpose of the experiment was to examine the relative impact of various forms of promotion

[1] U.S. Department of Agriculture, *Special Promotional Programmes for Winter Pears*. Marketing Research Report No. 611, July 1963, reported in *Experimentation for Marketing Decisions*, Cox, K., and Enis, B. (International Textbook Co., 1969).

on the sales of pears. The alternative forms of promotion were:

(a) Special point-of-purchase displays.
(b) Store demonstrations.
(c) Dealer contests.
(d) Media advertising programme.
(e) No promotion (control).

The test utilized five separate cities with a population of at least one million. Within each city, fifteen stores were chosen and all seventy-five were similar in terms of size and type of ownership, quantity of past pear sales, location and shopper type. The experimental design (a 'Latin Square') and test results are shown below.

5 × 5 Latin Square Design

Time periods	Cities				
	1	2	3	4	5
T_1	A	E	D	B	C
T_2	B	C	E	A	D
T_3	E	B	C	D	A
T_4	D	A	B	C	E
T_5	C	D	A	E	B

Sales of pears in seventy-five supermarkets
(over period of test)

Promotion type	Average sales per store per week (lb)	% change from control
A	227	− 12·7
B	323	24·2
C	317	21·9
D	225	− 13·5
E	260	—

Using Analysis of Variance, it is possible to see if the variation in sales is due to the areas chosen, to the time periods, or to the type of promotion. Thus the experimenter is able to say with a high degree of certainty how effective one promotion is relative to another. In this particular instance the variation due to the promotions was significant, and thus it was demonstrated for this product/market situation that store demonstrations and dealer contests achieved the best results in terms of sales amongst the promotional types tested.

Experimental approaches to promotional pre-testing have been reported for some time, but their widescale adoption has been slow. The expense and the complexity of experimentation is a major disadvantage, as is the very real possibility of competitors gaining foreknowledge of promotions and even intervening in the experiment to distort the results! In addition, the Latin Square type experiment described above does not allow for interaction between variables, which is often unrealistic.

Factorial designs are an experimental form which enable interaction to be assessed. They are generally more expensive to administer, and can become highly complex. A simple example of a two-factor design is given below. Here we are attempting to assess the interaction of below-the-line promotion with theme promotion, the intention being to ascertain whether the whole really is greater than the sum of the parts.

2 × 2 Factorial design

	B_1 Below-the-line promotional programme	B_2 No below-the-line promotional programme
A_1 Theme campaign	A_1B_1	A_1B_2
A_2 No theme campaign	A_2B_1	A_2B_2

These four combinations (or 'treatments') would have to be randomly assigned to a number of areas, preferably at least twenty, so that the experiment would be replicated five times during the test period (replication enables the precision of the results to be increased). In fact, to make the results more meaningful it would be necessary to have not just theme advertising/no theme advertising, and below-the-line/no below-the-line, but intermediate stages too.

The type of result that one might expect from a factorial design of this nature would take the form in Figure 8.9. Here we can see the effect of various combinations of theme advertising, and below-the-line promotion. Given that we could quantify these via a factorial design, it is relatively straight-

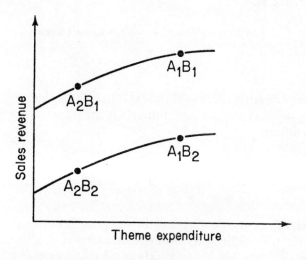

Figure 8.9

forward to compute the effectiveness of each input and the interactive effect, if any.

Let us say that the following hypothetical results were derived from such an experiment:

Sales effect of promotional interaction (£'ooos)

Theme advertising	Below-the-line expenditure	
	High (B₁)	Low (B₂)
High (A₁)	24	11
Low (A₂)	16	8

The increased sales resulting from spending more on below-the-line is computed as follows:

I

$$\frac{(£16,000-£8,000)+(£24,000-£11,000)}{2}$$

$$= £10,500$$

Similarly, the effect on sales revenue of a high level of theme advertising is:

$$\frac{(£11,000-£8,000)+(£24,000-£16,000)}{2}$$

$$= £5,500$$

and the *interactive* effect of above- and below-the-line promotion acting together to produce a total effect greater than the sum of advertising:

$$\frac{(£24,000-£11,000)-(£16,000-£8,000)}{2}$$

$$= £2,500$$

Apart from the problems of this approach outlined earlier, there is the additional problem of carry-over effects. It is known, for example, that the rate of sales for branded advertising products will decay over time if theme advertising is removed, but this may not be evident for some time (Figure 8.10). Thus, if an experiment is performed, perhaps of the nature of a switch from theme advertising to below-the-line, which produces its own effect on sales, then the researcher might be misled about the new treatment's effectiveness, thinking it to be superior to theme advertising, whilst in fact, the effects of the theme advertising were still operative.

In experimental approaches to pre-testing generally it is useful to follow a procedure something along the lines given by Kempthorne:[1]

(1) Statement of the problem.
(2) Formulation of hypotheses.
(3) Devising of experimental technique and design.
(4) Examination of possible outcomes and reference back to

[1] Kempthorne, O., *The Design and Analysis of Experiments* (Wiley, New York, 1952).

the reasons for the inquiry, to be sure that the experiment provides the required information to an adequate extent.

(5) Consideration of the possible results from the point of view of the statistical procedures which will be applied to them, to ensure that the conditions necessary for these procedures to be valid are satisfied.

(6) Performance of experiment.

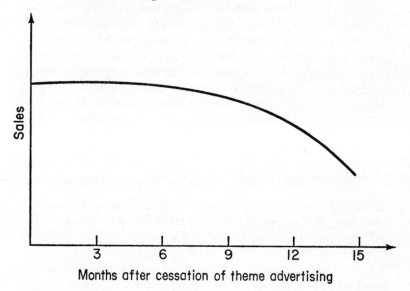

Figure 8.10. Sales decay curve for typical branded product

(7) Application of statistical techniques to the experimental results.

(8) Drawing conclusions with measures of the reliability of estimates of any quantities that are evaluated, careful consideration being given to the validity of the conclusions for the population of objects or events to which they are to apply.

(9) Evaluation of the whole investigation, particularly with other investigations of the same or similar problems.

POST-TESTING PROMOTIONS

In order that the problems encountered in setting up and

administering experimental tests of promotional effectiveness may be avoided, it becomes necessary to look at the possibilities for evaluation *after* the event. Post-testing of all promotional forms, for theme and below-the-line alike, is becoming increasingly sophisticated as the research technology available to the market researcher develops.

The basic problem in assessing promotional effectiveness is to determine what would have happened had there been no promotion. Now this can be ascertained via experimentation, but at a price, as we have seen. In fact, procedures exist for estimating 'what would have happened' by using a predictive device, which enables the researcher to then compare the actual outcome with the predicted outcome. One of the most powerful devices available utilizes the Negative Binomial Distribution (NBD) and its approximation, the Logarithmic Series Distribution (LSD).

USING NBD/LSD TO EVALUATE PROMOTIONS[1]

Assuming that we can measure the proportion of housewives who bought the brand in the period in question, and the average purchases made by a housewife in the period—information that can be derived from Attwoods, A.G.B. or T.C.A., for example—it is possible to be quite specific about purchasing patterns in the following period. In effect, we are using these two parameters to define the distribution of purchase frequency, and this distribution, it has been found, approximates very closely to the NBD/LSD for most frequently purchased consumer goods.

The researcher needs only to know the following quantities in order to make a prediction about what would have happened, given no promotional activity:

b: The proportion of the population buying brand X at all in the period.

w: The average number of times these buyers of brand X buy in the period.

---

[1] This section is based on A. S. C. Ehrenberg's 'Towards an Integrated Theory of Consumer Behaviour', *Journal of the Market Research Society*, Vol. 11, No. 4 (1969).

Now if in the next time period brand X is bought by a similar proportion of the population (b per cent) and at the same average frequency per buyer (w), there is no trend in sales, and a stationary or equilibrium situation for brand X exists. In general this b per cent does not comprise exactly the same purchasers of brand X in period two as in period one, and Ehrenberg[1] has demonstrated that the following relationship exists:

The proportion of the buyers of brand X in the first period who buy X in the second period is approximately $2 (w-1) (2\cdot3w-1)$, and that these repeat buyers buy brand X in each period with an average frequency of approximately $1\cdot23w$. Further, those consumers who bought brand X in period one, but not in period two (or vice versa) would buy it in the period in question with an average frequency of approximately $1\cdot4$, which is a constant. It can be seen therefore, that the magnitude of 'w', the average frequency of purchase, determines the repeat purchase pattern.

If, for example, buyers of brand X in a given period buy it on average three times, then under no-trend, equilibrium conditions about $2 (3-1) (6\cdot9-1) = 0\cdot68$ (or 68 per cent) of them are found to buy brand X again in the next equal period, and they do so on average about $1\cdot23 \times 3 = 3\cdot7$ times each.

We are thus able to postulate a 'norm' for the product in terms of repeat-buying. The next step in the evaluation is to observe the actual repeat-buying during the period of the deal. The difference between the two, other things being equal, may then be ascribed to the effect of the promotion.

Even so, we may not be able to isolate the promotional effects completely. For example, in the period under examination it may be that competitive promotional activity is abnormal. Again with many heavily promoted brands there is frequently an overlap of promotions and it is difficult to separate the effects of one promotion from another. Figure 8.11 shows a typical example of promotional activity for one brand over a number of four-week periods.

[1] *Op. cit.*

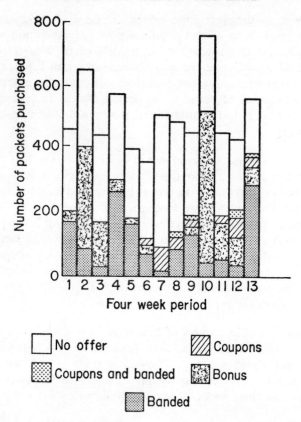

Figure 8.11. Example of overlapping and complexity of promotional activity (washing powders). *Source*: Attwood Consumer Panel, Great Britain.

USING CONSUMER PANELS TO ASSESS PROMOTIONAL EFFECTIVENESS[1]

A continuous consumer panel is a ready source of data on all aspects of purchasing behaviour, and this can often yield information on the effects of below-the-line promotion. Panels can be used as monitoring devices during controlled experiments, but they can also be used non-experimentally after the

[1] An excellent survey of the possibilities for the use of consumer panels in assessing promotional expenditures, on which this section is based, may be found in Parfitt, J., and McGloughlin, I., 'The Use of Consumer Panels in the evaluation of Promotional and Advertising Expenditures', in *ADMAP* (December 1968).

event to separate the effects of the promotion from the non-promotional sales effect. They may also be used for evaluating promotions on new products, a facility not available with the N.B.D./L.S.D. method. Parfitt and Collins[1] have described a method for predicting ultimate expected brand share of a product. The basic formula for this prediction is:

$$\text{Estimated penetration of the brand} \times \text{Repeat purchasing index} \times \text{Buying rate index*}$$

* Buying rate index is a measure of whether buyers are heavy, medium, or light buyers in the total market against the average of the market.

Parfitt and McGloughlin give an example of the effect of a price-cut promotion on an established brand of detergent (Brand X). The ultimate penetration of this brand was estimated at 20 per cent of all buyers in the market and it had a repeat purchase rate of 25 per cent (which the authors suggest is not untypical in a highly competitive, relatively disloyal market with five or six major brands to choose from) in effect producing a market share of approximately 5 per cent. A 50 per cent price-cut promotion was then introduced which increased penetration to 31 per cent (see Figure 8.12).

Depending on the repeat purchase rate, and the buying rate index of the new customers brought in by the offer, the ultimate effect on brand share of the promotion may be estimated in the following way:

	Ultimate penetration	×	Repeat purchase rate	×	Buying rate index	=	Ultimate brand share
Before introduction of offer	20%	×	25%	×	1·03	=	5·15
After introduction of offer							
Buyers before offer	20%	×	25%	×	1·03	=	5·15
Buyers after offer	11%	×	6%	×	1·01	=	0·65
							5·80

(*Source*: Attwood Consumer Panel, Great Britain)

The long-term effect of the promotion therefore was to

[1] Parfitt, J. H., and Collins, B. J. K., 'The Use of Consumer Panels for Brand Share Predictions', in *Market Research Society Conference Proceedings* (1967).

increase brand share by 0.8 per cent. In other words, the share increased by a factor of 12½ per cent resulting from a 50 per cent increase in ultimate penetration.

ADAPTIVE CONTROL OF PROMOTIONAL EXPENDITURE

Attempts at assessing the impact of a given promotional

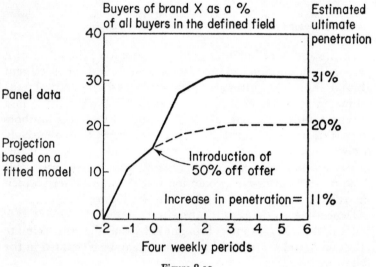

Figure 8.12

Source: Attwood Consumer Panel, Great Britain

expenditure are of little use if the results are not incorporated in promotional decisions in future time periods. We need therefore to integrate research feedback into the decision process: such a method we might call 'adaptive control'. Figure 8.13 illustrates the nature of the feedback loop.

In order that these 'optimal' expenditures may be determined, it is necessary to construct a model which will suggest possible sales response to different levels and types of promotional expenditure. Little[1] has suggested such a relationship in the following formulation:

[1] Little, J.D.C., 'A model of Adaptive Control and Promotional Spending', *Operations Research*, Vol. xiv, No. 2 (1966).

$$S = \alpha + \beta x - \gamma x^2$$
$$P_r = mS - x - c$$

where:

S = Sales rate (sterling value per household per year).

P_r = Profit rate (sterling value per household per year).

x = Promotional rate (sterling value per household per year).

c = Fixed cost (sterling value per household per year).

m = Gross margin per unit (percentage).

α, β, γ = parameters

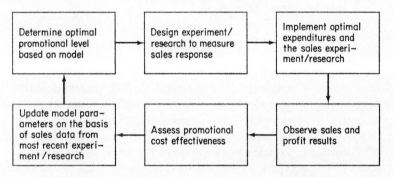

Figure 8.13. Cycle of adaptive control of promotional expenditure

Assuming a response curve exhibiting diminishing returns to promotional expenditure after a point, Little demonstrates by calculus that the profit maximizing level (x^*) of promotional expenditure is given by:

$$x^* = \frac{(m\beta - 1)}{2m\gamma}$$

The parameters of the sales response function (α, β and γ) are determined by experimentation and by interpolation. They will probably vary over time, and thus the necessity to have an adaptive approach whereby differences between the actual profit level and the level predicted are used as indicators of the validity of the parameters.

This is a simplification of a complex model, but it serves to illustrate the potential for applying a rigorous, scientific approach to the monitoring of promotional effectiveness and the adjustment of promotional expenditure. To enable such an adjustment to be made, the manager requires one or both of two things. He needs to know whether the original promotional objectives were realistic. Monitoring the environment to provide the information necessary for this approach may suggest that they were not. Second, given that the objectives are in fact sound, it is necessary for the manager to know if the deviation of actual from predicted is due to some temporary aberration in the marketing situation, or whether some more permanent change has occurred.

SUMMARY

In this chapter, promotional decisions have been placed in a framework of planning/control/adaption. The purpose of this type of sequence is to enable a more cost-effective stance to be adopted by marketing management in their planning and evaluation of below-the-line activity. It is not suggested that mathematical techniques can remove the need for managerial judgement or creativity in this area. Below-the-line promotion is far more of an art than a science at the present, and will probably continue to be so for some time to come. Rather, it is suggested that the application of rigorous procedures of the type that have been described in this chapter will enable the effectiveness of specific promotions to be more closely assessed.

However, it must be stressed that such an assessment of promotional effectiveness should not be made in terms of sales alone. In the same way that redemptions of promotional offers do not adequately reflect the sales effect of those offers, so, too, short-run sales increases do not necessarily reflect the long-term effect that the promotion may have on the brand. The problems of promotion/brand interaction discussed in earlier chapters lie below the surface of short-term sales curves, and are not easily discernible. The need now in promotional research is to create and discover the tools that will enable these longer-term effects to be exposed.

MARKETING BELOW-THE-LINE: SOME PROMOTIONAL FUTURES

OVER its chequered history below-the-line promotion has manifested many forms. Many established companies can record promotional activity stretching back to the turn of the century and further. In a way, the Victorian era was the great age of promotion, which, in all its forms, above- and below-the-line, was less restrained and certainly less truthful in its claims. Dubious and often outrageous properties were ascribed to the products being promoted and unsupported evidence of widespread use by the nobility and royalty was advanced in support of products ranging from corsets to laxatives.

Not every promotional form was artless or unsubtle, however, and Pears soap had a great success selling reproductions of Sir John Millais's 'Bubbles', which had virtually become their trade mark. Later years were to see incredible growth in the popularity of competitions; the era of the newspaper crossword with entries measured in tens of thousands was at its height between the wars. Other, more fanciful, promotions were sponsored by the newspapers, from Great Air Races to Lobby Lud.

The present promotional scene, whilst giving the appearance of frenzied activity, is, in comparison with earlier decades, quite clearly more restrained. Some of the constraints on promotional activity are institutional. For example, the Advertising Standards Authority very clearly defined the boundaries of promotional activity. In the case of premium promotions, for instance, the Authority lists the following requirements that should be met:

● Good faith should be shown in estimating the quantity of the goods on offer likely to be demanded.

● Goods on which an offer is made should not be sent out from the factory after the stock of premium goods is exhausted.

● The conditions of the offer should be visible to the customer before he or she purchases the goods.

Similarly, rulings exist for promotions aimed at children or competitions with 'socially undesirable' prizes. Other, legal, constraints exist in the form of the Betting and Gaming Act, 1963, and the Trade Descriptions Act, 1968. The effect of the Betting and Gaming Act has been to narrow severely the scope of competitions; if the competition is in fact a lottery, then this would make it illegal under the terms of the Act, and thus the deviser of a competition has to take great care in the construction of the rules. The Trade Descriptions Act has had its main impact on 'money-off' type offers. Here the law requires that the 'money-off' offer must relate to a price at which the product was originally offered, and this reduction must be a real one. Problems may also arise if the offer runs for some time, in that the new price could be interpreted to be the 'recommended price'. The Trade Descriptions Act also stipulates that where premium promotions are offered as being worth some sum of money, then they must actually be worth that amount if sold through the usual channels. Similarly, products offered in a promotion must match the description of them given in the offer.

Clearly the marketing manager involved in preparing a promotional programme now needs to take cognizance of a good number of external constraints on his actions. Indeed, the law is often confusing in these matters, and on several occasions in recent years successful promotions have had to be withdrawn as a result of court rulings clarifying the law.

External constraints aside, however, there are a number of forces at work which are circumscribing the activities of the promotional planner. In Chapter Five some of the behavioural undercurrents to consumer marketing were identified, and as a result of these, and other factors, there can be no doubt that the consumers' attitudes to the various forms of below-the-line promotion are changing.

It has been suggested that as the customer gains 'sophistication' in his or her tastes, that the more unsubtle promotion is going to have less of an impact, and even possibly a negative effect on purchase dispositions. At the same time, it is possible that the more creative and thoughtful promotion will gain increasing support. David Ogilvy once said that 'the consumer is not stupid—she is your wife'. Whilst this may not always have been true in terms of the sophistication of the consumer, it is certainly more the case now. People's life-styles change and with it their tastes for products; at the same time the product becomes more than a commodity in that the choice of brand will often reflect some aspects of the purchasers' personality. If the promotion fits in with this 'market personality' then well and good, but, as times change, so too must the promotion change to match the changed requirements of the consumer.

Not only is the consumer changing, but the companies and the products which they market are changing too. By the year 2000 it is almost a certainty that the mass of products being offered in most consumer markets will be products not yet created. They will be products that cater for changed tastes or for activities greatly changed from the ways they are performed now, for example, cooking. Increased discretionary income and more spending on items such as leisure activities will mean that opportunities for products as yet unthought of will arise. Changes in the profiles of markets are already foreseeable. By 1975, for example, there will be 17 per cent more people aged 10–14 and 7 per cent more aged 15–19 than in 1970. Together they will number nearly nine million persons, and will be 15 per cent of the population. This trend may well continue to the end of the century, providing a country populated in the majority by a youth-oriented society. And even with the present low rates of growth of real consumer income, the United Kingdom population's total wealth is forecast to rise by 25 per cent in real terms over the same period. Combine these changes with a general increase in education levels and it becomes apparent that there could be revolutionary changes on the marketing front long before the year 2000.

What do these likely futures hold for below-the-line promotion? It is certain that, to a very large extent, the future of below-the-line promotion is linked to the future of promotion generally. Advertising agencies, particularly those more sentient to change, are thinking already in terms of how they can meet the communication needs of the next thirty years. New products and new markets call for new means of communication. If agencies become more involved with a company's total communication problems, then there is every possibility that the present major role of below-the-line promotion may be reduced as it becomes less appropriate to changed marketing conditions.

The thesis that suggests itself, therefore, is that the present meteoric rise of below-the-line promotion has come about in response to certain, highly particular, market circumstances. There is no guarantee that these circumstances will remain unchanged, indeed the signs of change are already apparent. Thus in the same way that below-the-line promotion assumed its present proportions as a result of major developments in the trading and retailing environment—such as the abolition of Retail Price Maintenance, the rise of the supermarkets, and the concentration of buying power—so too, could it fall back to a level more typical, say, of the 1950s in terms of the percentage of total promotional expenditure.

Creatively, too, there seem to be limits to the development of below-the-line. Theme advertising can reflect and even anticipate changed societal values and cultural norms and thus adapt to new situations. It is unlikely that below-the-line promotion will be capable of this flexibility and adaptability.

Nevertheless, in the immediate short term it would be unwise to talk in valedictory terms about below-the-line; it still has a lot of mileage left in it, as its users continue to find. But the message of the future is clear; as market needs, and the products that meet those needs, change, so too must the promotional message change and, as a result, perhaps the medium too.

HOUSEWIFE QUESTIONNAIRE

Age of housewife:

Socio-economic class:

Demographic data:

Readership habits:

1. Thinking about your normal buying habits, where would you place yourself in the following scale in terms of economy?

Very economy-minded	Economy-minded	Neither economy-minded nor extravagant	Extravagant	Very extravagant

2. Where would you place yourself on the following scale in terms of adventurousness in trying something new?

Very adventurous	Adventurous	Neither adventurous nor conservative	Conservative	Very conservative

3. The following list gives an indication of some of the major forms of promotions used by manufacturers. Bearing these in mind, we would like you to make a choice between the following pairs of offers. Please indicate your choice by a cross (x) showing which you would choose if you had a choice. For example:

	Every time	Most times	More times	Neither or both equally	More times	Most times	Every time	
Offer A				x				Offer B

We would like you to choose your answer fairly quickly, as it is your immediate reaction to the choice between each pair in which we are interested.

	Every time	Most times	More times	Neither or both equally	More times	Most times	Every time	
Free sample delivered to your door								Extra quantity of same product, or sample of a different product banded to pack
A representative for the product calls at house offering prizes or entry to a competition in return for proof of purchase								Coupon
Free gift with product								Chance to enter a competition by buying product
Chance to send away for quality goods at a cheaper price								Free sample delivered to your door
Free gift with product								Money off
Chance to enter a competition								Coupon
Extra quantity of same product or sample of a different product banded to pack								Free gift with product
Money off								Chance to enter a competition
Free gift								Chance to send away for quality goods at a cheaper price
Coupon								Money off
A representative for the product calls at house offering prizes or entry to a competition in return for proof of purchase								Free sample delivered to your door
Chance to enter a competition								Extra quantity of same product or sample of a different product banded to pack
Free gift with product								Coupon
Chance to send away for quality goods at a cheaper price								A representative for the product calls at house offering prizes or entry to a competition in return for proof of purchase

Left item	Every time	Most times	More times	Neither or both equally	More times	Most times	Every time	Right item
Extra quantity of same product or sample of a different product banded to pack								Money off
Free gift with product								Free sample delivered to your door
Coupon								Chance to send away for quality goods at a cheaper price
Chance to enter a competition								A representative for the product calls at house offering prizes or entry to a competition in return for proof of purchase
Money off								Free sample delivered to your door
Extra quantity of same product or sample of a different product banded to pack								Chance to send away for quality goods at a cheaper price
A representative for the product calls at house offering prizes or entry to a competition in return for proof of purchase								Money off
Free sample delivered to your door								Coupon
Chance to send away for quality goods at a cheaper price								Chance to enter a competition
A representative for the product calls at house offering prizes or entry to a competition in return for proof of purchase								Free gift
Coupon								Extra quantity of same product or sample of a different product banded to pack
Money off								Chance to send away for quality goods at a cheaper price
Chance to enter a competition								Free sample delivered to your door
Extra quantity of same product or sample of a different product banded to pack								A representative calls at house offering prizes or entry to a competition in return for proof of purchase

K

Question 4
Could you estimate how many promotions of one sort or another
you have participated in during the last six months?

Question 5
Have you any comments on such promotions generally?

The survey of United Kingdom housewives was conducted during
October 1969, by Market Search Unit Limited, 121 Victoria Street,
London S.W.1 on behalf of Horniblow, Cox-Freeman, and the
University of Bradford Management Centre. Self-completed ques-
tionnaires were received from 1,012 housewives. The demographic
breakdown of the survey was as follows:

		Number in sample
Age group	16–24	90
	25–34	169
	35–44	178
	45+	573
Social class	A B C$_1$	349
	C$_2$D E	662
Working class	Full-time	211
	Part-time	172
	Non-working	629
Family	Children at home	394
	No children at home	616
Area	London and South-East	351
	South-West and Wales	163
	North-West	126
	North-East and North	150
	Midlands	131
	Scotland	90

The sample was constructed on a regional stratification and
respondents selected at random.

The attitudinal classification produced the following scores:

1. Thinking about your normal buying habits, where would you
   place yourself on the following scale in terms of economy:

Very economy-minded	Economy-minded	Neither economy-minded nor ex-travagant	Extravagant	Very extravagant

from which were derived:
    Economy-minded 69%
    Neither, nor   22%
    Extravagant   9%

2. Where would you place yourself on the following scale in terms of adventurousness in trying something new:

Very adventurous	Adventurous	Neither adventurous nor conservative	Conservative	Very conservative

from which were derived:
    Adventurous   49%
    Neither, nor   22%
    Conservative 29%

QUESTIONNAIRE TO DEALERS ON PROMOTIONS

CLASSIFICATION: Name of respondent:

Position of respondent:
Name and address of organization:

(a) Type of shop:
    (i) Multiple/Co-op.
    (ii) Symbol/Ind.
    (iii) Other Ind.

(b) Services:
    (i) Self-service
    (ii) Counter service
    (iii) Both

(c) Shopping area:
    (i) Primary
    (ii) Secondary

(d) Gross weekly revenue:
    (i) Under £750
    (ii) £751/£1,500
    (iii) £1,501 +

(e) Number of employees:
    (i) 1–10
    (ii) 11–50
    (iii) 51–100

Question 1

Below are a series of factors which may or may not have influenced your decision in evaluating a promotion offered to you by a manufacturer.

Please mark the line with a cross (x) in the place most appropriate to indicate the influence each factor would have on your decision.

(a) *Coffee*

Suppose a promotion offer was made to you for coffee; how much influence would the following factors have on your evaluation of the likely success of such a promotion.

	Much influence	No influence at all
Factors		
Product is a brand leader		
Rate of stock-turn		
Existence of own-label brand		
Percentage mark-up		
Amount of own time which will be taken up by promotion		
Amount of space taken by promotion and product		
Amount of inconvenience caused by promotion		
Value of promotion to the consumer		
Power to attract customers into the shop		
Offers currently running on other brands		
Amount of in-store display offered with promotions		
Amount of advertising planned to back the promotion		
Frequency of use of promotions by ʹbrand manufacturers		
Extent to which brand is advertised on TV		

(b) *Toothpaste*

Suppose a promotion offer were made to you for a brand of toothpaste, how much influence would the following factors have on your decision?

	Much influence	No influence at all
FACTORS		
Product is brand leader		
Rate of stock-turn		
Existence of own-label brand		
Percentage mark-up		
Amount of own time which will be taken up by promotion		
Amount of space taken by promotion and product		
Amount of inconvenience caused by promotion		
Value of promotion to the consumer		
Power to attract customers into the shop		
Offers currently running on other brands		
Amount of in-store display offered with promotions		
Amount of advertising planned to back the promotion		
Frequency of use of promotions by brand manufacturer		
Extent to which brand is advertised on TV		

Question 2

In this question, we are interested in the effect, in your opinion, that each type of promotion listed below has on your sales of a certain product type.

Please indicate the position nearest the effect, in your opinion, of each promotion by placing a cross (x) on the line.

(a) *Coffee*

What, in your opinion, would be the effect of the following promotions on sales of coffee:

	Great effect on sales	No effect on sales
PROMOTIONS		
Coupons to consumer		
Free samples distributed to consumers		
Money off to consumer		

Consumer gets chance to enter a
  competition
Dealer gets a cash discount
Quantity discount for dealer
Gift pack to consumer
Gift at check-out to consumer
Dealer gets free gift or chance to
  enter competition
On-pack offer of ⎫
  coupons   ⎬ On
On-pack offer of ⎬ next
  discount   ⎭ purchase
On-pack offer enables customer
  to send off for goods at a discount
Extra quantities in packets
In-store demonstration sampling
Free gift in return for proof of
  purchase
Re-usable containers
Personality promotions
Money back on proof of purchase

(b) *Toothpaste*
What, in your opinion, would be the effect of the following
promotions on sales of tootpaste:

	Great effect on sales	No effect on sales
PROMOTIONS		
Coupons to consumer		
Free samples distributed to consumer		
Money off to consumer		
Consumer gets chance to enter a competition		
Dealer gets a cash discount		
Quantity discount for dealers		
Gift on pack to consumer		
Gift at check-out to consumer		
Dealer gets free gift or chance to enter competition		

On-pack offer of ⎫
  coupons   ⎬ On next
On-pack offer of ⎬ purchase
  discount   ⎭

On-pack offer enables consumer to
 send off for goods at a discount
Extra quantities in packs
In-store demonstration sampling
Free gifts in return for proof of
 purchase
Re-usable containers
Personality promotions
Money off on proof of purchase

CONSTITUTION OF THE RETAILER SURVEY

The constitution of the retailer survey was as follows:

1. *Sample size and constitution*
The size of the sample taken was 423, being sub-divided into the
following demographic sub-sections:

(a) Type of shop:
  - (i) Multi/Co-op.   238
  - (ii) Symbol/Ind.   88
  - (iii) Other/Ind.   95

(b) Services:
  - (i) Self-service   294
  - (ii) Counter-service   124
  - (iii) Both   5

(c) Shopping area:
  - (i) Primary   252
  - (ii) Secondary   169

(d) Gross weekly revenue:
  - (i) Under £750   73
  - (ii) £751–£1,500   47
  - (iii) £1,510+   55

(e) ITV areas:
  - (i) London   70
  - (ii) Midlands   67
  - (iii) Granada   44
  - (iv) Yorkshire   77
  - (v) Central Scotland   38
  - (vi) Wales/West   29
  - (vii) South/South-West   51
  - (viii) North/North-East   23
  - (ix) East   24

(f) Number of employees:
    (i) 1–10   215
    (ii) 11–50   73
    (iii) 51–100   8

A quota sample of 500 retailers was designed and the placement and follow-up of the self-completed questionnaires was undertaken by Market Search Unit on behalf of Horniblow, Cox-Freeman and the University of Bradford Management Centre in January 1970.

CHECK-LIST FOR MANUFACTURER INTERVIEWS

INVESTIGATION OF BELOW-THE-LINE PROMOTIONAL ACTIVITY

These items are guide-lines for the interview. You should follow up any hopeful-looking leads which lie beyond what is specifically listed here, however. It may be helpful to begin the interview by explaining the purpose of the investigation and why the University is involved, and then lead into the topic by asking:

1. What does the concept of below-the-line mean to your company?

2. Why does your company get involved in this type of promotion at all?

3. Can you tell me the first occasion on which your company employed below-the-line promotional activity?

4. Do you view above- and below-the-line promotions as substitutes for one another? If not, why not? How are they able to offer something distinct?

5. What sort of budget procedure do you use for above- and below-the-line promotion?

6. What types of below-the-line promotion have you used in the last three years?

7. Do you see the various types of below-the-line promotion as working in different ways from one another or not?

8. Do you have specific objectives for particular below-the-line promotional activities? What sort do you have? Can you give some examples please?

9. Do you ever use below-the-line promotion in a defensive manner? If yes, under what circumstances?

10. Have you been able to track down any information outside of your own experience in below-the-line promotion? If yes, where, and what did you learn?

11. To what extent do you engage in pre-testing of below-the-line promotions? What methods do you use, and what results have you achieved? Were pre-test results borne out in the actual situation?

12. Who decides what the 'item' to be used in a below-the-line promotion will be? Can we pin it down to some recent examples?

13. What pattern of management for the below-the-line promotion do you use? Advertising agency's role, premium promotion agency, own company, etc. What are the arguments for and against this pattern of management?

14. How do you measure the success or otherwise of a below-the-line promotion activity? What yardstick? (Sales of product or redemption or both, and what else?)

15. What influences does the retailer have on the pattern of below-the-line activity in which you engage? Could you give some examples? Will you tailor-make a below-the-line promotion for a powerful retailer?

16. I would like to put two perhaps provocative ideas to you now which have been suggested as influencing the pattern of below-the-line promotion. I would be grateful if you would comment on them:

(a) It has been suggested that below-the-line promotion has become an absolute necessity because of the way in which so many highly branded goods have become no more than general 'commodities' in the customer's eyes. How does this view strike you?

(b) House labels and private brandings have made it more or less unavoidable that manufacturers will have to use below-the-line promotion.

Name and address of respondent

Title of respondent:

Company name:

Number of below-the-line promotions used in past 12 months:

(This study was conducted by researchers from the University of Bradford Management Centre amongst fifteen United Kingdom companies involved in consumer promotions in June 1970.)